O] WOMAN'S GUIDE TO LIFE

How to live a kinder, easier and more authentic life

Estelle Taylor

Copyright © Estelle Taylor 2024
This book is sold subject to the condition that it shall not, by way of trade or otherwise, be lent, resold, hired out, or otherwise circulated without the publisher's prior consent in any form of binding or cover other than that in which it is published and without a similar condition including this condition being imposed on the subsequent purchaser.
The moral right of Estelle Taylor has been asserted.

This book has not been created to be specific to any individual's or organizations' situation or needs. Every effort has been made to make this book as accurate as possible. This book should serve only as a general guide and not as the ultimate source of subject information. This book contains information that might be dated and is intended only to educate and entertain. The author shall have no liability or responsibility to any person or entity regarding any loss or damage incurred, or alleged to have incurred, directly or indirectly, by the information contained in this book.

For James Knox Taylor

CONTENTS

Introduction 1
Notes to Readers 2

Life 3

1.	It's your definition of success that matters 4
2.	Stop waiting to live 5
3.	You're in the driver's seat of your life 6
4.	Act on your hunches (and some ad-hoc dating advice that snuck in there) 7
5.	Get out of your comfort zone 8
6.	Everyone needs to feel seen 9
7.	It's okay that not all friendships last a lifetime 10
8.	Kindness is a multiplier 12
9.	Don't shy away from the bereaved 13
10.	Streamline your life 15
11.	Should I say it, or zip it? 17
12.	Staying safe in the jungle of life 18
13.	Be selective about who you spend time with 20
14.	Dialling down the intensity in a heated conversation 21
15.	Connecting people you know can sometimes backfire 22
16.	Do a life check-in (and yes, I love a car analogy) 23
17.	Take time to recognise your achievements 24

18.	Label less, investigate more	25
19.	Gob-shite behaviour is the domain of the unhappy	26
20.	Listen to your gut	27
21.	You don't need an excuse to celebrate life	28
22.	Photograph important documents	29
23.	The Christmas card hack	30
24.	Sending a physical letter is so retro it may even be cool	31
25.	When people are angry, it's not always about what you think it's about	32
26.	The interconnected pattern of life	33
27.	Take more pleasure from the simple things	34
28.	Living more sustainably	35
29.	Yes, I live here too	36
30.	The art of a good conversation	37
31.	Never underestimate the power of a hug	38
32.	The validation nudge	39

Body 40

33.	Listen to your body	41
34.	Stay strong and mobile for as long as possible	42
35.	Weight loss and maintaining a healthy weight	43
36.	Get things checked out; don't wait	46
37.	Managing menopause	47
38.	Balanced fitness	49
39.	Look after your teeth and gums	50
40.	Super supplements	52
41.	Ageing is relative	54

42.	The most effective things you can do for younger-looking skin	55
43.	Skin regime, night and day	57
44.	Treat your hard-working skin	59
45.	Easing sore muscles	60
46.	Embrace your gorgeous grey	61

Mind 62

47.	It's all about perspective	63
48.	Be aware of how you're expending your mental energy	65
49.	Oh, it's not important	67
50.	Have a chat with yourself	68
51.	Dial down the people-pleasing	69
52.	Make time for your inner child	71
53.	Stop expecting other people to act the way you think they should	72
54.	Recognise and replicate the fulfilling stuff	73
55.	You don't have to justify your beliefs	74
56.	Speak up; don't let things fester	75
57.	Good versus bad obsessions	76
58.	Why are you putting yourself under unnecessary pressure?	77
59.	Act before prolonged stress gets its foot in the door	78
60.	Breaking the cycle of cross-generational family dysfunction	80
61.	Staying connected to older relatives	81
62.	Counselling is for the good times as well as the bad	82

63.	Recognise the difference between fear and danger	83
64.	Face and treat those mental and emotional scars	84
65.	Stop being so hard on yourself	85
66.	Sometimes, you need to prioritise you	86
67.	Everyone needs a purpose	87
68.	Pick your battles	89
69.	If you want to move on, get good at forgiveness	90
70.	Be a light in the dark	91

Work 92

71.	How to ace an interview – applicants	93
72.	More than a contract	98
73.	Beware the toxic culture	99
74.	Don't get into email bunfights	101
75.	Feedback is your chance to become even more shit-hot	102
76.	To find the best solution, you have to dig	104
77.	Protect your time like a mama bear protects her cub	105
78.	Sorry, I f@cked up	107
79.	Avoid your manager getting blindsided	108
80.	Staying on the right side of your manager	109
81.	What's the 'So What'?	111
82.	Communications best practice	112
83.	Enjoyable presentations (yes, they can actually be engaging)	114

84.	Make summarising one of your superpowers	117
85.	Respect your experience	118
86.	Work is the most important thing in your life	119
87.	Making career moves	120
88.	Embrace change (or, my preferred title, Be the Polo Pony)	124
89.	When you're on holiday, be on holiday	126
90.	Be careful around Them and Us thinking	128
91.	Stop and lift your head up from the never-ending prairie that is your task list	129
92.	Walking the managerial seesaw	131
93.	Interview tips for managers	132
94.	Ruling through fear or trust	136
95.	Staying on the right side of your team	137
96.	It takes two to find a resolution	140

Finances 141

97.	Start a pension as soon as you start working	142
98.	It pays to make the big switch	144
99.	Do I still want this?	145
100.	Savings first	146
101.	Pay off the most expensive debt first	147
102.	Sometimes it's safer to ditch the credit card	148
103.	Make a Will, please	149
104.	Enduring power of attorney	152

Home 154

105.	Have a backup plan for getting into your home..... 155
106.	If there isn't a contract, clarify the details in writing... 156
107.	Easy-access kitchen storage 158
108.	Ditch the five-year-old tinned food (your home isn't an underground World War II bunker)........... 160
109.	Getting the most from your freezer 161
110.	The all-round, do-everything kitchen knife 163
111.	Hand-wash non-stick cookware 164
112.	Towels gone as rough as a badger's bum?............. 165
113.	Getting blood stains out of clothes 166
114.	When pillowcases go rogue 167
115.	Getting rid of water marks on wooden furniture... 168
116.	The great Anti-Squeak 169
117.	Bleeding radiators 170
118.	Maximising wardrobe space 172
119.	The big mattress flip 173
120.	House plants that are generally hard to kill........... 174
121.	Setting a hearth fire 175
122.	Safety lights at night.. 177
123.	Preparing for potential power cuts......................... 178
124.	Reducing electricity bills 179
125.	If you're considering photovoltaic (PV) solar panels.. 181
126.	How much sun will your garden, terrace or balcony get? 184
127.	A crash course in gardening 185
128.	Garden care over winter... 191

129.	Right for tight, left for loose	193
130.	Keep your bins inside your garden gate	194
131.	Selling your home	195

Travel ... 198

132.	An unapologetically nerdy packing list	199
133.	Making the most of the space in your liquids bag	201
134.	You can use a second liquids bag for prescription medicine	203
135.	Pack a Multi Charger Cable	204
136.	Empty the bins	205
137.	Pre-holiday home security	206
138.	Final checklist before leaving home	207
139.	Photograph your parking zone	208
140.	Getting through airport security	209

About the Author ... 210

Introduction

Life has its moments of wonder and joy as well as stress and pain. It's hard enough as it is without being overly hard on ourselves or others. If ever there were a time when we needed more peace, laughter, hope, tolerance and simplicity, it's now.

I was once described by one of my mentors as a reflector. Someone who mulls things over. This book is a summary of the things that have stood out to me the most over the last 40 years about interactions with others, being kinder to yourself and living a more authentic, peaceful life. Along with my thoughts around health, work, finance, home life and travel, with the aim of making life that little bit easier and happier. If I could do a download of useful learnings and hand it to my 20-year-old self, this would be it.

Wherever you happen to be in your life, if you read this and get just one useful thing from it, or if it reminds you of something you once knew, but had forgotten, then this book will have been worthwhile. I'm a firm believer that content finds its way to its reader.

Notes to Readers

1. Let's get this out of the way first. If you have any concerns about your physical or mental health, please speak to a medical professional.
2. Any products mentioned in this book are simply because I like them and use them. I have no affiliation with any products or brands.

You don't need to read this from front to back. Feel free to skip around, open random pages or read it from back to front, whatever floats your boat.

1

It's your definition of success that matters

One person's idea of what a successful life looks like might be very different from someone else's. For some, it's how far you climb in your career, how much money you earn, how much power and influence you wield. For others it might be how much free time you have, being able to work outdoors or having fewer responsibilities and less things to look after.

The point is, you're not living anyone else's life. Not your parents', not your manager's, not your teammates' and not your neighbour's. You're living YOUR life. What do you value the most? Think about what success means for you, what's most important to you, and start working your way towards that. Don't live your life according to other people's expectations. You don't have to follow the herd.

2

Stop waiting to live

There you are, thinking that things will be better or easier when this or that happens (whatever that is for you). That you'll be able to really enjoy life, focus on yourself more and do the things you want to do, at some undefined point in the future. No. You're wishing away your life. Stop waiting to thrive. No one knows how long we're here for. So live your life more today, enjoy what you can enjoy now and stop putting off the good stuff.

Living each day like it's your last? Very difficult to do. If you can do that, keep going. I salute you. Otherwise, choose one thing this week, month or year that you've been putting off for whatever reason or justification, but wanting to do for a while now. Something you know you'll enjoy. Build in regular nice things. Start small and work up to the bigger things if you need to (or just dive straight into the big stuff). Even if it scares you. In fact, even better if it scares you (as long as it's safe).

There's a big difference between just existing day to day, and living an enjoyable, fulfilling life, rich in experiences and interactions.

3

You're in the driver's seat of your life

You wouldn't get in a car and drive around for hours with no destination in mind (unless you just fancied doing that one day, for the heck of it). So why would you do that with your life? You're in the driver's seat of your life. So where do you want to go? What do you want your life to look like in three, five or ten years? Where do you want to be then, what do you want to be doing, who are you with, what does it look like and feel like?

You don't have to have it all mapped out, particularly if you're just starting out, but have a rough destination in mind for the next few years. Know what it looks like. If the decisions you're making now are being made with that destination in mind, you've a better chance of getting there. And a lot of the time, you will. Sometimes life throws a spanner into your plans, and sometimes you just feel like going with the flow, but it's still good to have an idea of where you want to go.

4

Act on your hunches (and some ad-hoc dating advice that snuck in there)

If you feel an internal nudge to go somewhere, check something, call someone you haven't spoken to in a while, take a course, go to an event or a talk, then do it. It could be a thought that's just popped into your head or something that's been at the back of your mind for a few days. Acting on those internal nudges has generally served me well, and I found something useful came out of it, either for me or for someone that I care about.

Just bear in mind, I'm talking about hunches that are likely to be in your best interests here. I'm not talking about messaging someone you went on a date with weeks ago who never got back in touch. It's highly unlikely that they had a death in the family or got hit by a freak asteroid. No contact, is a complete message in itself. Focus your time on those who think you rock. And while I'm on the topic – you're already complete. You came into this world complete. You do not need anyone to complete you. You can, however, choose to spend time with another whose completeness plays beautiful harmonies with yours.

5

Get out of your comfort zone

Like Bilbo Baggins in *The Hobbit*, comfortable at home with his pipe, books and slippers before he very reluctantly headed off on an adventure with a bunch of dwarves and a wizard, sometimes you need to push yourself out of your comfort zone and out of your usual routine. It's good for you. Do something challenging, unusual (for you) or scary (safely). It helps you feel alive, stronger and more confident. Plus, it can be a lot of fun.

6

Everyone needs to feel seen

I remember watching the movie *About Time*, when Tim (played by the wonderful Domhnall Gleeson), one of main characters, talks about travelling back in time to relive a day, to be really present for it. It struck a chord with me.

Those brief interactions we have with people day to day: the person at the till in the supermarket, the bus driver, the shop assistant, the courier, waiter or waitress, the barista. Having that human interaction is important for us. It might be very brief, but looking someone in the eye, saying hello, giving them a smile, maybe asking how their day is going, it makes a difference. For you, as well as them.

7

It's okay that not all friendships last a lifetime

It's not just okay, it's normal. You may have friends from school who remain friends all your life, and there's something particularly gratifying about having friends where you've known each other's history and family for such a long time. You'll probably also make friends through work or hobbies, because of where you live or other things that you have in common. While some of these friendships might be long-term, some may only last a few months or years. You'll simply drift apart from some over time, or your perspectives on life may diverge to the point where you start to clash.

Being friends with someone takes (worthwhile) time, effort and energy and you only have so much of that to invest. So don't be afraid of having a friendship cull every few years, so you can focus your energy on the relationships that are the most positive, healthy and balanced.

Does it feel good being around them? Are they supportive? Is it balanced, in that listening and support is a two-way street rather than one-way?

If you're making all the effort to keep things going or regularly feel drained or down after spending time with them, it may be time to have an honest chat or step back, temporarily or permanently.

8

Kindness is a multiplier

One small, or large, act of kindness, consideration or patience ripples out to affect many more people than the original giver and receiver.

If the motorway is practically at a standstill, people are trying to join it from a feeder road and you slow down to make space for one of them to join, the person you made space for (and the person in the car behind you) is more likely to do the same for someone else in the next few minutes.

It's not just a short-term, in-the-moment thing either. The ripple can be felt many years later. If you had a teacher, trainer, supervisor or colleague who treated you kindly, you're more likely to treat your trainees, your team or your new colleagues like that in the future. Because you remember how it felt.

With each considerate act, you're putting more (good) things in motion than you realise, affecting more people than you think and for some, the impact could last a lifetime.

9

Don't shy away from the bereaved

You're thinking, *They probably need time alone to grieve, I shouldn't bother them at a time like this.* You may not know what to do or say, and maybe a part of you would rather put a little distance between yourself and death, even if that's a subconscious reaction. The problem is, if everyone takes that approach, you end up with someone who's dealing with grief, huge adjustment, possibly a lot of paperwork, and now they really are on their own.

If you check in with them, ask them how they're doing, and they say, 'I'm not ready to talk about it just yet. I need some space for a few days,' that's one thing. But more often than not, they will want to talk about how they're doing and feeling; they will want to talk about the person they've lost and share memories with someone else who knew them.

So do reach out, check in regularly and give them time and space to talk about it. Help with the paperwork if you're a trusted friend or family member and they'd like some help. Help them to keep busy and get out and about if that's what they'd like to do, and be patient.

10

Streamline your life

Wherever you can, streamline your life to reduce the number of things that need to be remembered, looked after or done. For example:

1. Have a tag in your car to auto-pay motorway or highway toll charges
2. Consider astroturf if you don't have the time or inclination to mow grass
3. Check out robotic vacuum cleaners or mowers
4. Schedule your food deliveries from a local supermarket, using a saved online shopping list of the things you typically buy, that you can re-use, whether having your shopping delivered or shopping in person
5. Use local parking apps to pay for parking (and extend your parking remotely)
6. Pay bills by direct debit
7. Set alarms on your phone to remind you of things you need to do, like take medication, or bring someone to the doctor
8. A video doorbell will let you speak to couriers and agree on where to leave a parcel if you're not home, so you don't have to drive to the local parcel depot to retrieve it later

9. Back up your phone, your contacts list and your laptop or computer regularly to avoid time spent trying to retrieve or recreate important data

11

Should I say it, or zip it?

If you're ever wondering whether or not to tell a friend, family member, colleague or neighbour something that you heard, saw, read or was told, something that could be a little contentious, use the Constructive vs Destructive test. Will saying this be positive, useful or constructive for the person I'm telling? If yes, then say it. If the answer is no, there's nothing useful or constructive and it will only hurt, upset, annoy or create further division, then don't say it.

And, while we're on the topic, if saying something will help to boost someone's confidence, their personal growth, or just put a smile on their face, it's worth saying.

12

Staying safe in the jungle of life

I'm talking about situations where you feel under threat physically here. Firstly, listen to your intuition. It evolved as part of the human condition for a reason – to help us stay away from danger and survive.

The priority, where possible, is to avoid being in a situation where you feel under threat in the first place. So, if that person, group of people or situation is making you feel nervous or uncomfortable (even if you're not quite sure why) and you don't feel safe, either don't go there or get out of there. If something doesn't feel right, it probably isn't. And don't let peer pressure, social niceties or a perceived need for politeness sway you otherwise. There's only one person responsible for your personal safety (unless you're a minor), and that's you. Don't take any risks with it.

Your body language is important. Human predators aren't so different from animal predators in the way they choose their targets. So, when you're out and about, stand tall, put your shoulders back, bring your head up and look calm, confident (not aggressive), like you know exactly where you're going, and be fully aware of what's going on around you.

Everyone, women and men of any age, can benefit from a good self-defence course. That weekend course could just save your life.

13

Be selective about who you spend time with

Whether it's friends, colleagues, classmates, neighbours, family or extended family, spend most of your time with people who are positive, supportive and whose company feels good and empowering. And where possible, limit (or cut if you think it's the right move) time with those who leave you feeling drained, used, down or undermined.

14

Dialling down the intensity in a heated conversation

If you're in a situation where someone is agitated, annoyed and talking loudly to you or shouting, a natural reaction can be for you to raise your voice, too. If you do, you'll just drive the intensity upwards. It doesn't have to be like that.

If you can keep your voice quiet and calm throughout, there's a good chance they'll start to come back down to something closer to your lower, calmer voice. You're directing the intensity downwards and can hopefully conclude the conversation in that vein.

And if that doesn't happen, and they're continuing to shout, you can always take yourself out of the situation and say that you'll speak to them when they're not going to shout. And if at any stage you feel like things are unsafe, don't hang about to try this approach; get out of there.

15

Connecting people you know can sometimes backfire

If you have a friend who has an item or can provide a service that one of your other friends happens to be looking for, it can be tempting to put them in contact with each other.

It may work out fine and both parties will be happy with the outcome. But if anything does go wrong, you can end up caught in the middle of the crossfire, in a 'no good deed goes unpunished' kind of way. I've experienced two instances of this, one involving a puppy for sale and one involving drawings for an attic conversion. And I learnt that sometimes it's safer to let people find their own suppliers and solutions, and stand over their own choices.

16

Do a life check-in (and yes, I love a car analogy)

Your car (unless it's new) gets a health check every one to two years. In Ireland, it's the NCT. In the UK, it's the MOT. And that's just your car. How often do we have a check-in on our lives?

This can be done in under 30 minutes, as frequently or infrequently as you like.

Get a piece of paper, draw a big circle on it, then mark out eight segments, like a pie. Write one life category on each segment: Family, Friends, Health, Work, Home, Finances, Leisure/Fun, Personal Growth/Spirituality. You can change the categories, have fewer or add more. Score each category out of 10, depending on what's happening in each and write a few notes to summarise that. What's in good shape (getting scores of 7-10), what needs more attention (scores of 1-6) and what could you do to change that?

A quick life check-in can give you useful insights into what's working or not working well in your life, what could be done to redress any imbalances and bring your attention to the things that you hadn't stopped long enough recently to even notice.

17

Take time to recognise your achievements

Make note of what you've achieved each year. And don't downplay it – if it feels like an achievement for you, then it is. Write it down so you can look at it for years to come, because if your memory's anything like mine, you'll forget a lot of it. Life is busy. It's easy to just keep going without ever taking stock. When you do, it will often be a surprise, in a good way, realising exactly what you've done and achieved in the last few months. Take a moment to reflect on it.

18

Label less, investigate more

You may dislike, or even abhor someone else's views, beliefs or actions, but when we stick a label on someone and take no time to consider what brought them to that point, that action, or that way of thinking, we become further away from any possible understanding, de-escalation (if there's been anti-social behaviour or violence), resolution or change for the better.

19

Gob-shite behaviour is the domain of the unhappy

It's not that they're out to get you. While that's possible, it's thankfully uncommon. The way they're acting is a reflection of what's going on with them and it's much more about that than you. If they're unhappy, angry or resentful about things going on in their life (or past), it's going to leak out in their dealings with others. So just keep this in mind and try to cut them some slack.

And if this is someone you have regular contact with, and it's bringing you down, you can try and have a chat. Pick the right moment, when there's privacy, time and the mood seems right. Keep it constructive and factual, e.g. "When [.......] happens, I feel [.......]. Would it be possible to [.......] instead?" And failing that, look for ways to limit contact.

And I concede that some people who act like this are not unhappy. They're just being a bit of a gob-shite, which we all have the capacity to be.

20

Listen to your gut

Your body has a built-in, sophisticated security system. Call it whatever you're comfortable with – intuition, gut feeling, good feeling about, bad feeling about, a level of general hinkyness. Whatever you call it, sometimes it's trying to tell you something. Listen to it.

If something really doesn't feel right, if you can, act on it. Don't choose that supplier; don't hire that person; don't join that company; don't buy that item; don't make that decision yet; don't go in there.

You get the drift.

21

You don't need an excuse to celebrate life

The most precious gift you'll ever receive is your life. Billions have lived their lives and are now gone. Trillions are yet to be born. But you're here, alive in the world, right now. You already won the life lottery.

22

Photograph important documents

Take a photograph of your passport, driving licence and car registration and save them to a photo album on your phone. There'll be times when you need to access those details, even if you're not travelling, and it makes finding them quickly a lot easier. I've had my car for years and I still couldn't tell you the number plate details off the top of my head.

23

The Christmas card hack

If you're someone who likes to send Christmas cards, doing this makes the job a lot faster.

Once you have your Christmas cards written, with names and addresses on the envelopes, spread them out on a table so that you can see every address. Take one photograph of the collection (more if they won't all fit into one). Save the photo to a Christmas card photo album on your phone. Next year, just write the names on each envelope, then find that photo and you'll have all the addresses in one place, ready to add.

24

Sending a physical letter is so retro it may even be cool

Email and instant messaging are great. They're fast, practical and convenient. But there's nothing like the surprise of getting an actual letter or card in the post. It engages every sense – sight, hearing, touch, even smell (if you gave it a spritz of something nice before you posted it)

If you want to say something special, express how much you appreciate someone, say sorry or reconnect with a friend you'd lost touch with, consider sending a physical letter or card. It makes a much bigger impact.

Sometimes, old-school is cool.

25

When people are angry, it's not always about what you think it's about

If someone is angry about something that happened recently, it might be about that specific situation and nothing else. Just remember that sometimes, what they're actually angry about is something that happened before. It could be days, weeks, months or even years ago. They're still annoyed about that, and this latest thing is just the most recent irritation. It's been bothering them for a while now and they may not have raised it with you at the time, because people often shy away from confrontation, or saying what they really want to say.

Keep that in mind when someone's level of anger seems out of proportion to what just happened. It might be a different or longer-term issue that needs to be discussed and resolved. Along the lines of, "What's really annoying you here? Is it [.......] or is it something else?"

26

The interconnected pattern of life

I believe that there's a bigger, more complex pattern in life. Like a giant rug with millions of strands, where certain strands are meant to touch at specific points in the design.

When I look back over the years, it feels like certain people came in and out of my life at specific times, for just a moment or a longer period, so that I could either help them, or they could help me. It's funny how the universe lines things up based on what you or someone else is going through at the time. That interaction can be to support, validate a decision or give a nudge in a certain direction. It is, at least, how I like to think about life, and it gives it more meaning for me.

27

Take more pleasure from the simple things

The natural world is happening all around you, often unobserved. A row of birds lining up on a wall; friends laughing together in a park; dogs play-bowing; a mini cyclone of leaves.

Take time to stop and look around you. To notice and absorb it. It feels good and it can improve your day, every day. It can also be when you'll get some useful insights into what's going on in your life, how you feel about something, what you want or don't want. You need to allow some space for that, which isn't jam packed with entertainment. Time for observant daydreaming.

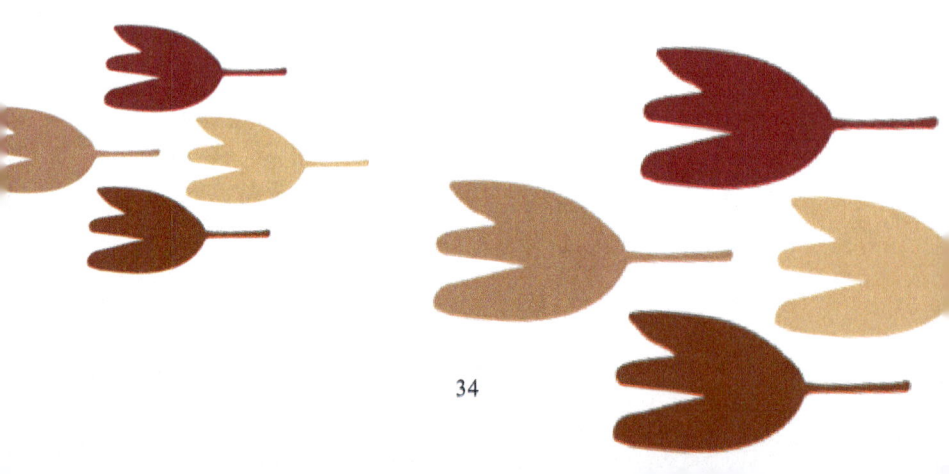

28

Living more sustainably

A friend of mine mentioned that she'd be reducing the number of flights she was taking, as one element of living more sustainably. At the time I thought it was a little extreme, but it has stayed with me. And just 12 months later it didn't seem extreme at all. I found myself making different choices too. It's a mindset shift.

I'm making a start on recycling more than just glass bottles, paper and plastics. Today, I'll make a new cover for my ironing board rather than order an entire new board. I still love to travel but I take fewer flights than I used to. Throwing things in the waste bin used to be the default action. It's now the exception. I'm selective about adding to my stuff – choosing lasting quality over quantity.

29

Yes, I live here too

Stop apologising for everything, for just existing (yes, sheepish one, you know who you are). You have just as much right to be here as anyone else. Anyone.

So, stop trying to take up the smallest space possible. Take up some space. Stretch out a bit. Make your presence felt. Think of it as the mental equivalent of doing a few virtual jumping jacks.

30

The art of a good conversation

Good conversations are like a tennis match where people take it in turns to gently lob questions and answers back and forth over the net to keep the game going. It shouldn't feel like one person is doing all the asking and the other person is doing all the answering, otherwise it gets boring very fast for the questioner, and for the answerer it can start to feel like an interview or an inquisition.

Be an attentive listener, make eye contact and don't be looking over their shoulder to see who else is there to talk to. It needs to be a roughly equal split in terms of who's asking the questions. Aim to be talking no more than 50% of the time, so the other person gets a chance to share things.

31

Never underestimate the power of a hug

If you think a hug would be welcome (it's safer to ask if it's someone you don't know well), hugs punch way above their weight when it comes to giving someone some moral support, showing that you noticed what's going on with them and care. One small act, one big boost of feel-good energy. If someone has had a bad day, if they're looking tired, quiet or down, a hug can help tip the day over into something more bearable.

In short, the world needs more hugs. Go forth and hug (with permission, and if it's in line with local tradition and social norms, and if you don't currently have some horrible lurgy).

32

The validation nudge

If there's something you suspect that a family member, colleague or friend would like to do (or do more of), and you think it would be good for them, ask them about it. And if it's what they'd like to do, encourage them to do it.

There are many reasons people may not reach for what they really want, or stop doing something they don't want, or no longer want to do. A sense of obligation, fear of seeming selfish, concern about other people's reactions or just not wanting to rock the boat.

Bringing it up and encouraging them, if it's what they really want to do, can be the small nudge that helps them have the confidence to make the change. To give themselves permission. So don't just think it. Say it.

Body

33

Listen to your body

Bodies can generally deal with a high level of stress for a short period of time, but when that stress is there for weeks or months, that's a different matter.

We tend to pay more attention to the warning lights on our car's dashboard than the warning signals coming from our bodies. Oil light on? Let's get that sorted. But if we're getting regular headaches, back pain or poor-quality sleep, we often just keep on going regardless.

Mentally, if you're going through one or more stressful things in your life, you may genuinely think, *I'm doing okay, I'm managing.* But if, during a prolonged period of stress, you're starting to get physical symptoms, e.g. digestive problems, palpitations, psoriasis, headaches or back pain, it's possible your body is saying, 'Well, you might think you're okay but I'm telling you, something needs to change.' Whether your symptoms are due to stress or something else, get things checked out by your doctor.

You might have a number of cars over the course of your life. You only get one body.

34

Stay strong and mobile for as long as possible

I remember watching one of the short movies at the Banff Film Festival about a free climber in his 70s. He had the body of a fit 30-year-old. I also remember being on a walking holiday in beautiful Jordan in my 30s, surrounded by people in their 60s and 70s who rang rings around me in terms of aerobic fitness and physical endurance.

If you keep asking your body to be mobile, flexible and strong, through the activities you do, you're more likely to be able to keep doing those things for longer. The less you use your body or ask of it, the less it becomes able to do, and you'll limit your mobility and independence. While you do have to respect your personal circumstances and capabilities (and doctor's advice), being much less physically able as you get older is not a foregone conclusion.

Don't reduce your activity levels as you get older; maintain or increase them.

35

Weight loss and maintaining a healthy weight

When my mindset is in the right place and I'm committed to getting my weight back within my preferred healthy range (if I've indulged in a few too many Maltesers), this is what works for me. But first, one caveat – everyone has different health considerations so do get advice from a doctor, dietitian or nutritionist before making significant changes to your diet.

Getting ready:

1. No surprise here, I cut out or significantly cut down on bread, pasta, rice, potatoes and high-calorie snacks like cake, biscuits and chocolate.
2. And to be ready for the times when I do have a craving for something sweet, I buy in small bags of sweet and salty popcorn, protein balls with cacao, and apples so I can slice them up and have them with a little peanut butter.

3. I keep a bottle of a kefir yoghurt drink in the fridge, to have a glass if I'm hungry between meals.
4. I start taking a supplement of chromium and cinnamon, which may help manage sugar cravings.

Breakfast options:

1. Two poached eggs over sliced avocado on half a toasted pita bread.
2. Two scrambled eggs with some herbs de Provence, chopped tomatoes and half a toasted pita bread.
3. Grapes or blueberries with yoghurt and some granola.
4. Two Weetabix with milk.
5. Two slices of porridge bread with jam or marmalade. This bread is so easy to make (thank you to my friend Shaunna for recommending it). Just search online for 'Mary Flahavan's Porridge Bread' for the recipe. Adding in some banana and almonds works well.
6. Hot porridge oats with Alpro hazelnut milk, adding a teaspoon of honey, some dried cranberries, pine nuts and some cinnamon.
7. An Almased protein shake. When I start the day with this, I find it easier to eat lighter meals for the rest of the day.

Lunch and dinner options:

1. I have what I think of as my Base Salads:
    A. Lettuce leaves, tomato, cucumber, olives, pine nuts (or whatever nuts you like) avocado and coleslaw.
    B. Rocket/arugula leaves, tomato, cucumber, grapes and a few dried cranberries. A slightly sweeter option.
    C. Lemon and mint couscous (you can buy microwavable pouches) served cold with cooked sweetcorn, kidney beans and chickpeas mixed in.

Choose one of the salads and add your preferred dressing. I mix in a tablespoon of minty tzatziki dip, Greek yoghurt, ricotta cheese or cottage cheese. Serve with some extra protein e.g. roast chicken, chicken goujons, chicken Kiev, sausages, bacon bits, avocado, goats' cheese, feta cheese or halloumi.

2. If I don't fancy a salad, and to increase my intake of vegetables, I'll often just cook a bowl of petit pois peas, green beans or sweetcorn, then add some crumbled feta or goats' cheese and bacon bits or ham.
3. A two-egg, tomato and mushroom omelette, if I didn't have eggs for breakfast.
4. And if I don't fancy any of the previous options:
   A. Four Schar gluten-free crispbreads with hummus and feta cheese on top (with a dash of green pesto). Or
   B. Four Nairn's gluten-free rosemary and sea salt flatbreads with avocado and sliced tomato on top (with some balsamic drizzle).

And beyond that:

I maintain or increase activity levels. Just a 30-minute walk in the park is good for you, physically and mentally.

Having the right mindset, recognising and dealing with triggers and not falling back into bad habits are the hardest parts long-term. To find something that is an ongoing way of life rather than a temporary diet. There are lots of companies who specialise in helping with that, as a group or through an app. It's a case of finding which kind of support or system works best for you.

What seems to be working for me is building more of the meal options mentioned here into my regular diet. Creating healthier meals that you genuinely enjoy makes it easier.

# 36

Get things checked out, don't wait

You know your body better than anyone else. If something doesn't seem right or changes and it isn't normal for you, don't be afraid to get it checked out. You'll either get the all-clear and be told it's okay and you can stop worrying about it, or if it is something that needs to be dealt with, the sooner that happens the better. Catch things and deal with them early for the best outcomes. Don't put off getting things checked out. Go and see a doctor.

37

Managing menopause

A few weeks before turning 51, I started to become very forgetful. I'd make arrangements to meet someone for dinner, or make an appointment, and completely forget about it until someone rang me to find out where I was, at which point I'd be sitting on the sofa feeling mortified. I lost my mental clarity; it was difficult to make decisions and everything felt muzzy. I felt very down, anxious and my ability to cope with stress, any stress, seemed to fall off a cliff. Suddenly, things that had never seemed daunting before, felt stressful. It took very little for me to feel overwhelmed.

It was only when describing this to a friend, who then asked me what age I was, that I realised it could be related to the menopause.

There are over 30 different symptoms of menopause - physical, mental and emotional, and what one-woman experiences can be completely different to another. For me it was primarily mental and emotional, with only a few physical symptoms.

Some of these menopause symptoms can be surprising. Most people are familiar with night sweats and hot flashes but there are many more, some of which you might not associate with menopause. These include, among others, joint pain, tiredness, racing or irregular heartbeat, anxiety, depression and trouble sleeping.

If that's happening to you, talk to your friends and family about what you're experiencing so they can support you, and speak to your employer if you're struggling at work.

Have a chat to your doctor if you're finding menopause symptoms a challenge (not every woman does). You can also discuss Hormone Replacement Therapy (HRT) with them, if you'd like to, and find a solution based on your personal circumstances and medical history. HRT got a bit of a bad reputation when it first came out, but research and data since then have provided a more balanced and accurate picture of benefits versus risks.

HRT doesn't just help to alleviate menopause symptoms; it can also help to reduce your risk of osteoporosis, heart disease, and maintain muscle strength.

It can take a few months to feel the benefits of HRT. For me, the forgetfulness and brain fog cleared within a week. It took a few months for my mood to improve and anxiety levels to go down.

38

Balanced fitness

When it comes to your physical fitness, try and include a mixture of:

1. Cardio fitness for your heart, e.g. running, swimming, a racket sport or dance (dancing is also particularly good for brain health)
2. Maintaining muscle and bone strength, e.g. lifting weights, walking, hiking or climbing
3. Maintaining joint flexibility and balance, e.g. yoga, pilates or tai chi

As you get older, you should be maintaining or increasing your hours of exercise per week, not decreasing them just because you're getting older. Older does not have to mean slower. You might just need to adjust your exercise to lower impact options that are gentler on your body, like walking, swimming, yoga or dancing.

39

Look after your teeth and gums

Ask your dentist about the right dental care for you and how often you should come in for check-ups and professional cleaning. Most of us like to eat, right? So you need to look after those puppies, and there are plenty of things you can do to look after your teeth:
1. Brushing twice a day with a fluoride toothpaste is good, but it doesn't clean between the teeth. Regular brushing on its own only does part of the job.
2. Floss (tape-style floss is less likely to get caught on fillings or crowns than a string floss) or use interdental brushes (like the TePe brand) once a day to clean between the teeth. Ideally, employ both. With a little trial and error, you'll find which sizes of interdental brush work for you (they should be snug but easily movable).
3. Brush with a toothbrush *after* flossing or using an interdental brush.
4. Bleeding gums means you need to floss or use interdental brushes more, not less, which can feel counter-intuitive. Don't skip days. The bleeding should reduce in a few days. If

it doesn't, see your dentist or dental hygienist. Receding gums can't be reversed, so try to keep them happy.
5. A good electric toothbrush is more effective than a manual toothbrush.
6. Don't rinse your mouth with water after brushing, you're just getting rid of all traces of toothpaste and it's better to let the fluoride have longer to work on your teeth.
7. Get a teeth guard if you grind your teeth or clench your jaw while asleep. And if you're doing that, you may want to have a look at your stress levels.
8. It's not so much about the quantity of sugary drinks or food that you eat that causes decay. It's more about the number of times per day you have them. Have your sweet food or drink in one sitting, if possible, rather than spread throughout the day.
9. Sticky toffees or a mouth full of jellybeans do not play well with crowns.

40

Super supplements

Let me kick this off by saying that a good choice for one person, may not be a good choice for someone else. So speak to your doctor about what supplements make sense for you and your medical history.

A good multivitamin can help balance out any vitamin or mineral gaps that aren't being fulfilled through a varied diet, which is the ideal scenario. For example, if you don't eat fish, you might want to consider a fish oil supplement, but you can also get omega-3 fatty acids through ground flaxseed, flaxseed oil, chia seeds or walnuts. These fatty acids support heart health and can reduce inflammation, among other things.

It can be difficult to get enough vitamin D from sunshine, so make it a habit to take that as a supplement or as part of a good multivitamin. Vitamin D isn't just good for bone health, it also helps your immune system fight off viruses and bacteria.

Magnesium is an important mineral that helps the body use vitamin D (which impacts your ability to absorb calcium). It helps your muscles and nerves to function normally, supports healthy enzyme function, energy levels and sleep. Plus it helps the nervous system, reducing the level of cortisol in your body and improving your ability to cope with stress.

Probiotics support gut health, and that can be boosted significantly by packing as many varieties of fruit and vegetables into your diet each week as you can. The more colours, the better. As well as having an impact on your physical health, a happy gut can also have a positive impact on your mood.

41

Ageing is relative

Like taxes, age comes for all of us. It has its pros and cons. Are you getting older and noticing those few wrinkles, the expanding waistline or things generally getting sore or heading south? I'm here to tell you, it's all just a matter of perspective.

Imagine you're visiting an elderly relative in a nursing home. You might be in your 40s, 50s or 60s. The people in the nursing home are in their late 70s, 80s and 90s. Those nursing home residents are going to take one look at you and consider you a youngster. They'll wish they were as young as you. You with your smooth skin, mobility and general springiness. It's all relative. Not feeling so old now, are you?

42

The most effective things you can do for younger-looking skin

The biggest skin ager is the sun's ultraviolet (UV) light. The sooner you adopt good habits to protect your skin, ideally from your teens onwards (when your parents are no longer slathering sunscreen onto you) the more you'll reap the benefits as you get older.

A minimum of Sun Protection Factor 'SPF' 30 in winter (face, ears, neck and the top of your head if you're a gorgeous baldy) and SPF 50 in summer. I love Reimann's P20 Sensitive Face sunscreen, which lasts up to 10 hours with one application.

Stay away from tanning salons, and if you can, stay out of the sun during the hottest part of the day (10am – 4pm). Enjoy the heat but sunbathe under an umbrella in the shade. If you are out in the sun, use a hat, cover up with light layers and keep topping up the sunscreen.

Being inside a car or bus with the windows closed does not protect you completely from UV rays, so use an SPF suncream when you're travelling too.

Protecting your skin from the sun isn't just great for keeping your skin looking good, it's significantly reducing your risk of skin cancer.

And if you want to look tanned, there are plenty of great self-tanning lotions and sprays out there. Go to a salon or get yourself a good tanning mitt (one with a wide band and a mitt on either end, so you can do your back). Exfoliate and put some moisturiser on your heels, ankles, knees, elbows and knuckles beforehand.

43

Skin regime, night and day

For years, if I went for a facial, the beautician would look at me with gently reproachful eyes and ask me about my skin regime, which was essentially, cleanse and use a moisturiser with SPF. They suggested other steps, involving a toner and serum. At the time I thought, *Nope. It's going to take too long. I don't have time and my skin will be overloaded.*

Eventually, mid-40s, I finally gave in and started following the steps they suggested. And found that it didn't take a long time to apply and my skin wasn't overloaded. In fact, it absorbed everything very happily, felt much softer and looked better. I've continued ever since.

For the evening, these are the steps for face and neck:

1. Cleanse
2. Spritz of toner
3. Serum
4. Moisturise

For the morning, it's the exact same regime, with one extra step, to protect your skin from UVA and UVB rays during the day:

1. Cleanse
2. Spritz of toner
3. Serum
4. Moisturise
5. SPF sunscreen (or just use a moisturiser that contains an SPF) with a protection factor of 30 or more in winter and 50+ in summer. Don't forget the tips of your ears

Then whatever make-up you usually use, if you use it.

44

Treat your hard-working skin

While the focus tends to be on the face and neck when it comes to skincare, the skin on some very hard-working parts of your body, like your feet and hands, can be lucky to get any attention at all. Even your car gets given some oil occasionally.

After your shower or bath, or before bed, put some moisturiser on your hands and elbows, knees, shins and feet, which can all get quite dry. Even if it's only once or twice a week. I love Aveeno Daily Moisturising Body Lotion.

45

Easing sore muscles

Just ran a marathon, spent all day digging in the garden or started a tough boot camp fitness class? If your muscles are screaming at you the next day or the day after, and you're finding it hard not to walk like John Wayne, run yourself a warm bath, lob in a generous handful of magnesium flakes and have a good soak. The magnesium will help to relax your muscles, assist with muscle recovery and ease some of the discomfort.

46

Embrace your gorgeous grey

If you want to stop battling with your grey roots and embrace your natural colour, do it. Don't listen to the doubters, if there are any. See how it turns out. You don't know what it's going to look like until it's grown out. There are lots of different shades of grey and patterns of colour in Mother Nature's salon.

If you love the colour, great. It can be a much more flattering colour for your face as you get older. Make sure your hair gets some extra care and conditioning going forward. A purple (toning) shampoo can also help to keep your natural colour bright. And if you don't like it, you can always go back to dyeing it. You have absolutely nothing to lose.

You may need to incorporate more colour on or near your face if your hair is much lighter. If light grey or white clothes suited you as a brunette or blonde, it may make you look a little washed out when you're grey. If so, bring more colour through in your make-up, jewellery, clothing and accessories.

Mind

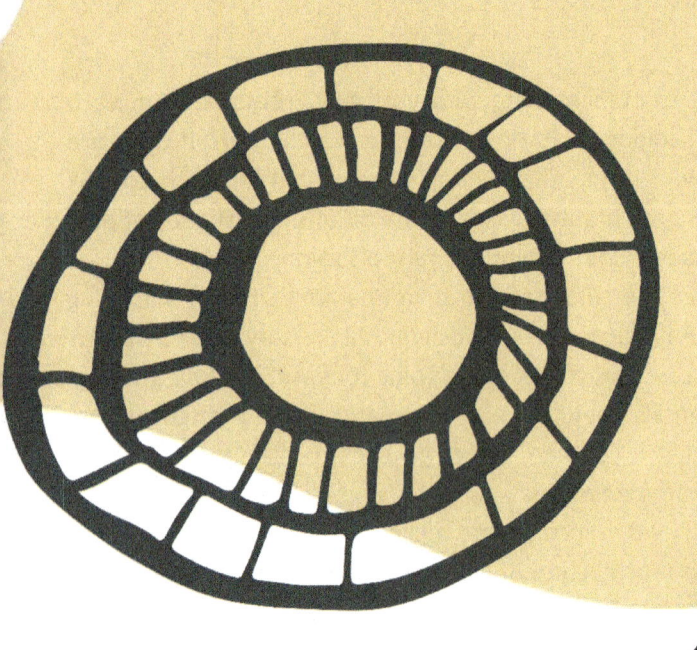

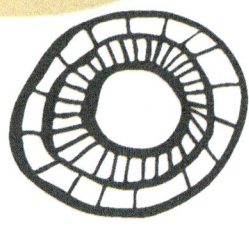

47

It's all about perspective

How you choose to see things, to frame the things that you experience, is a really important factor in your happiness and contentment. Two people could experience the exact same thing, but the way they'd tell that story could be so different as to be unrecognisable. The glass half full or half empty view of the world has power; it has an impact on your mind, body, health and happiness, for good or ill respectively. You can either make your mindset work for you or against you.

Focus on the learnings, positives and anything constructive that came out of things and don't assume that someone's behaviour, actions or decisions were aimed at hurting, ignoring or hampering you. It's possible, but it's just as likely to be down to other factors and nothing to do with you. They might be completely oblivious.

Try to just go with the flow if things are happening in the moment that you can't change, like a traffic jam or delayed flight. You can choose to get more and more wound up and angry, or you can choose to surrender to it and let go. You know which one is better for you. There are plenty of things we need to fight for, to rail against and try to change, but in a world of increasing stresses and factors outside of our control, we need to get better at knowing when to surrender.

48

Be aware of how you're expending your mental energy

Your mind, like your body, can get tired as the day goes on. Sometimes the topics running through it can be exhausting. Start to become more aware of what you're spending your time thinking about and whether it's useful, constructive and feels energising or relaxing. Or whether it's the opposite. Your mind doesn't have to run you.

If you're starting to fixate on past conversations, potential future conversations, negative things that might happen or wondering why someone is doing something, or not doing something – notice it and try to get off that particular mental treadmill and break the cycle:

1. Go and do something physical, e.g. a hobby, something fitness-related, a food shop, etc. Something that requires some level of concentration and physical co-ordination, so you're focussed on doing rather than thinking.

2. You can take the Park It approach: Hang on. This may never happen. Let's park it. I'll tackle that one if it happens.
3. If it's late at night and affecting your sleep, write down some notes about what's on your mind. It's not always negative thoughts keeping you awake. It could be ideas you have for a creative project you're excited about. It's often easier to get to sleep once you've offloaded that information by writing it down.
4. If it's something you're anxious about, ask yourself: If this actually comes to pass, what's the worst that could happen? How bad is that in reality? And what can I do about it that's under my control or influence?
5. One of my Dad's favourites was this: Is this still going to be an issue in two weeks' time? If not, acknowledging that it's a short-term thing can help gain some perspective on it. Soon, you'll be on the other side of this.

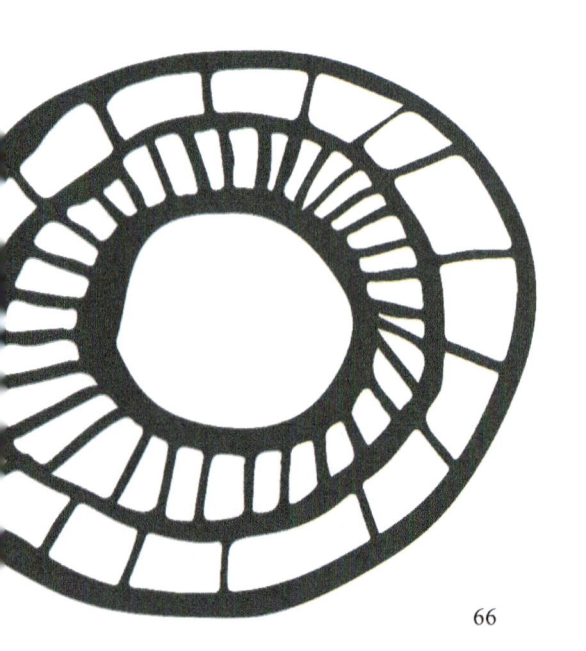

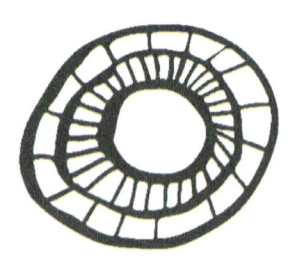

49

Oh, it's not important

If you're talking to a friend, colleague or manager about something, and you hear yourself saying things like, 'It's not a big thing, but...' or, 'It's not that important, but...' and generally downplaying it – is it just a minor issue? If you're needing to talk to someone about it and get it off your chest, it's probably not as minor as you're making it out to be.

It was important enough for you to feel the need to raise the topic and talk it through with someone. So give it its due. It's bothering you and possibly pushing one of your buttons. Discuss it, see if you can uncover what's bothering you the most about it and why, if that's not already clear.

50

Have a chat with yourself

I don't mean the *'I really need to cop myself on'* kind of chat. If you're feeling a certain way, you're aware of it, but you're not entirely sure why, then try having a chat with yourself. Ask yourself:

1. What exactly am I feeling here? Angry, frustrated, resentful, hurt, sad or something else?
2. Where is this coming from?

Either internally in your head, or write down the questions and see what comes out in the answers. I find writing it down is more effective. It can help you get some useful insights that wouldn't occur to you quite so clearly otherwise. And if you know what you're feeling and what's causing it, you can potentially do something about it. Or, just identifying what's going on and why, can be enough.

51

Dial down the people-pleasing

Yes, we're raised to be nice, to go with the flow, to think of others and that's fine. It helps society to function smoothly, but there has to be a balance. You have to make room for your needs and preferences as well as that of others. If you're starting to feel resentful, angry, unhappy, overloaded or that you can't be yourself, then you need to start making a few changes:

1. Say how you're feeling and ask for help from your family, friends or colleagues.
2. Agree what the priorities are if you're feeling overloaded.
3. Is this meeting or social invitation really something that you need to attend or want to be at? Can one of your colleagues or a family member be the representative who attends?
4. Compromise more with family and friends:
    A. I'll go to [50% or whatever] of these events or get-togethers going forward.
    B. Use the 'take it in turns' approach, e.g. 'We can spend this holiday with your parents, the next with mine and

the one after that we go somewhere we want to go or just stay at home.'

C. Spread the load, e.g. 'I organised the [whatever it is] for the last two years, someone else can look after the next one.' And don't step in and take over if it's not being done exactly the way you'd do it, or you'll only sabotage the assertive step you just took.

Use your words. Set boundaries. Start taking back some time. Take steps to deal with the things you're feeling resentful about.

52

Make time for your inner child

Yes, you're an adult. That doesn't mean you always have to be in serious adult mode. You do still have an inner child and it feels good to reconnect to that sometimes (preferably regularly). Hop onto that swing you just walked by (if it looks sturdy enough). Take the option to take the slide down, on that thing you just spent time walking up. Roll down that grassy hill. Sleigh down that snow-covered slope. Get involved in children's games, or just dig your old childhood games out of the attic if you still have them and play them with your friends.

Spend more time in play (okay, get your minds out of the gutter, people. I wasn't talking *Fifty Shades of Grey* here, but if that works for you, go for it). What I mean is, don't abandon your capacity to have fun and lose yourself in that. Didn't you used to be great at that? Life is serious enough as it is; it needs a counterbalance. Give it the counterbalance.

53

Stop expecting other people to act the way you think they should

You're just setting yourself up for disappointment, unnecessarily. They're not you. They haven't had the same upbringing and life experiences and thoughts as you, even if they grew up in the same family. They're making decisions from a completely different baseline, and there's nothing wrong with that (unless they're setting out to hurt themselves, others or being deliberately destructive, which is a different conversation).

In general, take it that people are just going about their lives, doing the best they can, making decisions based on their experiences and current situation. Accept it for what it is and them for who they are. If something is bothering you and you think there's an opportunity to influence their behaviour, go for it. Otherwise, accept that they're just doing them, while you're doing you, and that's as it should be.

54

Recognise and replicate the fulfilling stuff

Have you been feeling happier or more energised recently? Did you get a kick out of something you did or created? I get a lot of fulfilment from creating something tangible. For you it might be building, designing or writing something creative, art or crafting, joining a choir, volunteering, playing music, coaching a team or creating video or film content.

Have a think about whatever it is for you and try and build more of it into your life.

55

You don't have to justify your beliefs

If you have a different belief or opinion about something than someone else, you don't need to spend time trying to bring them around to your way of thinking, or justifying your standpoint. Leave it be. It's not a good use of your time or mental energy, unless a) you're in a debate team, b) someone is genuinely asking you about your views in a calm and respectful way, or c) you've chosen to pick this particular battle to make a point. Otherwise, you don't need to get drawn into potential verbal wrangles.

>Them: I don't believe in [.......] because of x, y and z...
>You: OK.

They're allowed to have their views and you're allowed to have yours. You may not agree with each other and that's fine. People will make up their own minds about things. Their views may or may not change over time, but that's for them to work through. That's their journey.

56

Speak up; don't let things fester

If there's something that's really weighing on you or bothering you and it's not going away, get it out there. Calmly, respectfully and assertively. Say it face to face or write it down if that's easier.

"I feel [.......] because [.......]"

"Can we make some changes, please? Would you be open to [.......]?"

"I wanted to say sorry that I [.......]"

Speaking up isn't a guarantee that things will change the way you'd like them to, but at least the anger, guilt, hurt or resentment won't keep building up in you, like a ticking time bomb.

If the other person is open to what you're saying, and there are changes you'd like to see, be ready to articulate that.

"What I'd like is [.......] Would that be possible?"

57

Good versus bad obsessions

Obsessed about a new series you're binge-watching or binge-reading? Okay, I'm not talking about that. That's fine. Unless you fell asleep and missed your train stop or faceplanted your lunch the next day, in which case you might want to look at that.

I'm talking about when you start obsessing about something you want and can't have, for whatever reason, and it's making you unhappy, angry or frustrated.

If you can take steps towards what you want, and it will simply take time, that's great and probably won't feel so bad because you're able to take some proactive action.

If that's not currently an option, and there's no external action you can take to make it happen, then you have to recalibrate how you're looking at this. It's either that, or more self-imposed frustration. Turn it on its head. Write down everything you're grateful for now and why; all the positives of your current circumstances. Do everything you can to love and appreciate the life you have today. It's a much nicer place to be.

58

Why are you putting yourself under unnecessary pressure?

You have goals and things to work towards? Great. But there are times when you're so busy progressing a few things at once, that you can lose sight of what really has to be done right now, and what doesn't.

If it's starting to feel stressful or overwhelming, and there really isn't an urgent deadline for every task, park the things you don't need to do right now. Why put yourself under more pressure than you need to if it isn't feeling good?

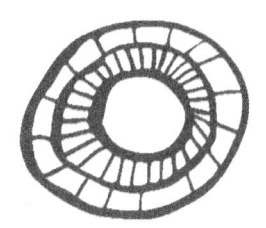

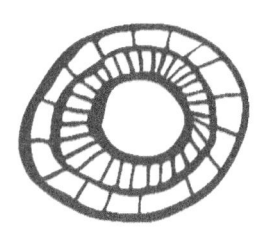

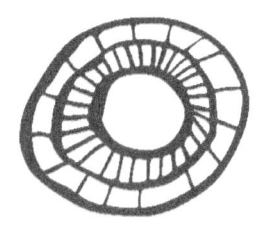

59

Act before prolonged stress gets its foot in the door

People can usually deal with a small to high level of stress for a short period of time, and a small amount of stress can help with performance and focus, e.g. an upcoming exam or speaking in front of a crowd. But dealing with a medium to high level of stress for a prolonged period, for weeks or months, is a whole other ball game. It's not sustainable.

The human body was built to recognise danger and either fight or run away from that large sabre-toothed cat or angry bear. It was intense, but short-lived. They weren't still running from that bear three months later.

If you're experiencing prolonged stress over a period of weeks or months, at some stage it's likely to start showing up in mental and/or physical symptoms, e.g. psoriasis, digestive problems, difficulty sleeping, palpitations, back pain, reduced appetite, lethargy, depression, forgetfulness or inability to focus. If you're experiencing something like that, but preferably before you get to that stage, recognise that this is your body and mind's way of saying, 'Hey, listen to me now, enough's enough, something needs to change.'

Talk to someone you trust – your partner, your manager or colleague, a good friend or sibling. Get those symptoms checked out by your doctor. Ask for help and find a way to make some changes to reduce whatever's causing that stress. It may involve difficult decisions, but no job, goal or commitment is worth that level of prolonged negative impact on your health.

You get one incredible, high-tech body and it comes with a (hopefully) super long warranty. You can't get a new one if you break it, but you can usually change your job, your relationships and your personal circumstances.

60

Breaking the cycle of cross-generational family dysfunction

Our insecurities, fears, triggers and general messed-upness (we all have something) come frequently, but not solely, from our childhood. Parents don't get a detailed manual on how to rear a child. They do the best they can.

If you think you have a mindset, trigger or negative self-belief that's holding you back from a happier life, speak to a counsellor if that's an option for you. I believe everyone would benefit from some counselling.

And keep in mind, if one or both of your parents struggled with something because of how they, in turn, were raised, that can affect the way they raised you. So certain dysfunctional elements can end up being passed down the generations. If you do get counselling to work through your challenges and understand them better, you have a better chance of breaking that pattern of behaviour when it comes to your children. You can break the cycle.

61

Staying connected to older relatives

If your parents or grandparents are older and living on their own, particularly if one spouse has passed away, there are lots of ways to help them feel more connected.

Set up a WhatsApp family group to share messages and photos. If this is your kind of thing, you can also use that WhatsApp group to take it in turns choosing a start word for Wordle, so that family members can do Wordle as a group and compare results afterwards. I warn you, it can get a little competitive (ahem, Janet). There's also Dordle, Connections, Quordle, Words with Friends and others.

For those further away or in another country, you can also do weekly video calls with children or grandchildren.

There are plenty of apps and games to help stay more connected in a fun way and counteract loneliness. It's not just good for older relatives; the connection is good for you too.

62

Counselling is for the good times as well as the bad

You don't have to be sad, grieving or really struggling to benefit from counselling. Go when you're well and work through your stuff when you're in a stronger place mentally and emotionally, because it's not an easy process. Go when you feel well and build up some resilience. Don't leave it until you feel like everything's coming apart.

Would you wait until every warning light was lit up on your car's dashboard before taking it to a garage? There are legally enforced checks that need to be done on your car on a regular basis, to help keep it safe and roadworthy. Think of an investment in counselling like a roadworthiness check for your mind and wellbeing – getting things sorted before they get worse or cost even more.

63

Recognise the difference between fear and danger

If you're afraid because your life is in danger and you need to take steps to protect yourself, that's one thing. That's real and you need to do something.

But there's a big difference between that and fear of something that might not ever happen. Do what you can to mitigate that fear, but then move on. Agree that you can cross that bridge if you happen to come to it, but you'll think about it at that point. Not now. Because you have much better and more constructive things to do with your mental energy.

64

Face and treat those mental and emotional scars

Most people carry around multiple hurts, from childhood and on into adulthood. Things you may have packed away in a box in your mind or heart, and then put a sturdy lock on.

Whether or not you've forgotten about them, or never fully saw them in the first place, they're still driving some of your decisions, some of your beliefs about yourself and others, and it's very likely to your detriment. If that belief, pattern or triggered action is limiting you, you can work on it, understand it better, change what you believe to be true and change your beliefs and actions. You can either do this through self-work, or through booking in with a professional.

65

Stop being so hard on yourself

Would you speak to your best friend the way you speak to yourself? Or would you be much kinder and more supportive to a friend than you are to yourself?

So stop beating yourself up and putting yourself down. It doesn't achieve anything useful. Go to counselling if you think it's due to a deeper self-belief that you need help working through. Otherwise, cut yourself some slack. Life can be tough, so be as kind and understanding to yourself as you'd be to your best mate.

You rock. You may not think so right now. But you do.

66

Sometimes, you need to prioritise you

You can't put everyone else's needs before yours all of the time. It's not sustainable and if you don't look after yourself, soon you won't be able to look after anyone. You might be treating everyone else around you generously and kindly, but you're not being kind or generous to yourself. Why not?

Your needs, your time out, you being prioritised and looked after – fight for it. You deserve that on a regular basis too. It doesn't make you a bad person, it makes you a healthier, and hopefully happier person.

67

Everyone needs a purpose

If you're stopping work for a period of time or retiring, you still need a purpose, for your own health, happiness and longevity.

Let's think Fred and Wilma Flintstone for a moment. In nomadic Stone Age tribes, every member probably had a role, whatever their age, and a way to feel useful and fulfilled. Whether that was hunting and gathering food, preparing food, finding shelter, raising young, looking after the sick, keeping the fire going or being a tribal elder.

We're living in a very different society today, but the drive of tribe life, pride in being useful, needed and having a sense of belonging and connection is still there. We still need to feed that need.

Whether that's volunteering; teaching your grandchildren to fish; raising pedigree pooches; coaching a youth sports team; growing prize watermelons; learning a new skill or language or mentoring someone who's interested in something you know well – find your thing. Having a reason to exist, in a way that feels rewarding and fulfilling, helps you to stick around for longer. Plus, it's more fun.

And maintain as many social connections with people per week as you can. In our long history of evolution, we've always been tribal and social to survive, not loners. It's one of the ways we thrive.

68

Pick your battles

Back to the point about being careful when it comes to how and where you spend your finite mental energy day to day. You don't need to be a constant feisty fighter. That's exhausting. What do you really need or want to take a stand on, and what can you choose to let go? Let certain things be non-stick. Just let them slide off you. It's not just for frying pans.

69

If you want to move on, get good at forgiveness

You can't move on from something painful, into a place even approaching serenity or happiness, until you forgive yourself and let go of the guilt, shame or damage caused. If you don't, you're keeping the door shut to other good things that could come into your life. You're saying, 'I don't deserve this good stuff, because of what I did.' Nothing good comes from that, only more destruction. There's already enough of that in the world. Everyone has hurt someone. Learn from it, move on and forgive yourself. Say it, a few times, after me, 'I forgive myself for [.......]'

Just as important, and possibly less considered, you also can't move on into a happier place unless you can forgive someone who's hurt you. Or at least forgive their actions, however awful they were. If you don't forgive the other person and you're still angry and hurt about what they did, you stay intrinsically tied to them, and it holds you back. Forgiving them isn't saying that what they did was okay. It's saying that you're ready to free yourself from that toxic link. You're forgiving them so that *you* can move on.

70

Be a light in the dark

If you're going through very dark times. If you feel unloved, unimportant, overwhelmed or if life feels pointless – reach out to someone you trust, or your local support group, and tell them how you're feeling.

Reaching out to someone is not an act of weakness, it's an act of strength.

And if you're feeling like that and reading this, take it as a strong reminder from the universe that:

1. You are loved.
2. You are worthwhile.
3. You are more precious than the rarest metal because there is one and only one of you in the entire world.
4. You are meant to be here, in this place and at this time.
5. The world and the people in it need you. You have a role to play.

There is always light in the darkness, if you look for it. Believe it. And if you can, be a light for others in the future, because you know what this feels like and the importance of having someone to talk to.

Work

71

How to ace an interview – applicants

This relates to general company interviews and not to the hiring processes of the tech giants, which is highly tailored and a whole other ball game.

It depends on the role, but generally an interview is not just a conversation or a getting-to-know-you situation. It's a verbal dance. Tactics will be applied, certainly from the employer's side, and there are also tactics that you can use. The ultimate goal of a successful interview is that you both win. You find the role that you want, and the company gets the person that they want. It's a harmonious match for you both.

This is what's going through the interviewer's mind:

1. Have they the experience, skills and ability to do this job?
2. Will they fit in with our culture and way of doing things?
3. Will they fit in with the existing team?
4. Are they likely to cause me any headaches or problems?
5. Do they genuinely seem to want this job, in this company?

6. Do I get a good feeling about them and can I picture them working here?
7. Are they likely to stay long enough to make the training-in period worthwhile?
8. Do they stand out from the crowd (in a good way) in terms of their attitude and approach?
9. Can they problem-solve and think on their feet?
10. Are they going to be a good ambassador in terms of how they represent us?

Your pre-interview preparation:

1. Make sure you've found the correct company (that can be tricky if it's a large group using the same brand) and have a good look through their website, their most recent press releases and social presence. That's your insight into their activities, culture and what's important to them. Make note of what stands out. The more you can talk accurately about their business during the interview, the more seriously you'll come across as wanting the job.
2. Look over the details of this job vacancy so that it's fresh in your mind. Particularly if you're doing multiple interviews for different roles in the same week.
3. Have answers prepared for the tricky questions, e.g.:
    - What's your biggest weakness/development area? Choose something true to you that has an element of upside, e.g. a tendency towards perfectionism; the fact that you know you need to delegate more; a desire to train in a new, up-and-coming skillset.
    - What do you know about this job? (See point 2 above.)
    - Why do you want this job? Your answer needs to tie in your experience, career aspirations and personal values, with the role, goals and values of the company and why it's a good match.

- Why do you want to leave your current role? It's safer not to criticise a previous employer or manager, even if you have just cause. Make it more about your career plan and the kind of experience you want to gain next.
4. If it's the kind of role where you can showcase past work, then bring some examples with you.

During the interview:

1. Turn your phone to silent.
2. Be able to give a concise summary of your CV (one to two minutes max). They don't need the detail, they already have your CV. They're mostly just checking that what you sent and what you're saying matches, and whether you can be focussed and concise. There are more important things to spend interview time on.
3. Listen well to what they're asking, saying and how they respond to what you're saying. That's giving you cues about what's important to them and you can use this.
4. If you're not clear on a particular question, ask them to clarify. It's a better use of their time and yours.
5. If they ask towards the end of the interview whether you have any questions. Yes (hell yes), you have questions. This is probably the most useful part of an interview for the applicant. It's your chance to show your interest, your knowledge of their business and stand out from the crowd. There are two types of questions you can ask: 'let me impress you with my outstanding candidacy' type questions, and 'housekeeping' questions around the interview process or logistics of the role. Choose 4-5 max. You don't want to over-grill them, unless they seem super chatty and happy to continue, which is a good sign.
6. Good 'let me impress you' questions include things like:
   - If I were successful in getting the role, what would the priorities be for first six months? (AKA, I'm goal oriented

and keen to get started). The other beauty of this question is that it gets them imagining you in the role, and you definitely want them doing that.
- What are the company's main goals in the next twelve months? (AKA, so I can get behind this plan too.)
- How would you describe the culture at [company name]? (AKA, I'm curious about the day-to-day vibe.)
- What's the management and leadership style at [company name]? (AKA, how am I going to be treated by my manager?)
- What do existing employees like most about working here? (AKA, go on, sell yourselves to me.)
- What are the opportunities for learning and development? (AKA, because I care about improving myself and you will then benefit from my mad skills.)
- What is the company's approach to sustainability? (AKA, do the company's values align with mine?)
- You mentioned [.......] earlier, can you tell me more about that, please? Choose something they seemed proud of or excited about, but only ask if you're genuinely interested, otherwise it will show. (AKA, I really was listening to you and if this is important, I should know more about it.)
- When [....... product/service] that you mentioned earlier is launched, who's the target market and how is that being developed?

7. Good 'housekeeping' questions include:
- Can you tell me a little more about the team this role would be in?
- What's the next stage of the interview process?
- May I ask how many others you're interviewing for the role?
- When are you hoping to have someone in place? (If you're not currently working, this is an advantage that

you can highlight, because you can start immediately, while someone else may be working their notice period.)

8. Salary and benefits. My advice would be not to raise the topic of salary and benefits, unless they specifically bring it up. Save that for when you're in a much stronger negotiating position, i.e. if offered the role. If they ask in the interview what salary you're expecting, you can keep your options open by giving them a range, e.g.: "I'm looking for [……., your minimum happy, realistic figure] to [……., the previous figure plus 10-20%]. I'm sure we could find common ground there but I feel the best time to talk salary is when there's an offer on the table, so let's see how things go." They will internally applaud your restraint and patience. If things seem to be going particularly well and they've given you a few 'buying signals' one after the other, you could ask a cheeky, 'Are you offering me the role?' with a smile and see what the response is.

Post-interview:

If you thought the interview went well, you liked them and the sound of the company and the role, and you think they liked you, you could always send a short email or message to the interviewer(s) to say you enjoyed the interview, you're very interested in the role and you look forward to hearing the results of the selection process. It's quick, easy and can be one more thing to help you stand out from the other candidates. And if it didn't seem like a good match, just chalk it down to interview experience. Interviewing well is a skill in itself.

72

More than a contract

Work is a contract in more ways than one. There's the employment contract, and there's the unspoken contract.

The employment contract gets looked at for a few minutes (mostly to check your salary, annual leave and working locations) and then gets filed away. What stays every day after that (while you're working for them) is the unwritten business relationship and emotional contract, which is just as important.

Work is not only about what's in it for you, or for them. It's a two-sided thing. You both want something from the other, you both need each other.

Like any good relationship, the unspoken contract between you and your employer should include a fair and reasonable balance of give and take, mutual support, flexibility, respect, empathy and trust. It works better for both sides when you play nice and have each other's back.

73

Beware the toxic culture

In one of my very first jobs, there was a lovely gentleman who'd been off sick for a number of weeks. He called once, to let the CEO know that he wouldn't be coming back to work for a few more weeks yet. I ended up intercepting that call. I offered to transfer him to the CEO a couple of times during the call but he was adamant that he didn't want to speak to him directly. He practically begged me to just pass on the message. I remember thinking at the time, that it seemed a little odd.

A few months later, I realised that I was starting to feel physically sick at the prospect of going into work. I was also working closely with the CEO. I can't remember any one particular reason why I felt like that. I think it was a wide combination of factors. I was lying on the bed, curled up feeling nauseous before going to work, which was not normal for me, and it was a wake-up call.

I started applying for other jobs that same week and thankfully got the hell out of Dodge not long afterwards and into a much healthier environment. I don't think that CEO ever set out to create a toxic culture. He may have been unaware. It's possible he had a very stressful life, at work and/or at home. But if you're experiencing something like that, you don't have to stick around.

Try to get a sense of workplace culture at interview stage. But if you've just started a new job and notice a combination of some of these signs, a warning bell should start ringing in the back of your mind:

1. Little engagement in team meetings. People are quiet, reluctant to speak up (put their head above the parapet) and when they do say something, there's a good chance either they or someone else will be shot down or criticised.
2. There's a culture of high pressure, blame and pointing fingers.
3. A higher-than-average number of sick days or other absenteeism in the team or company.
4. A high turnover of staff.
5. A manager that's passing onto you and your teammates, the criticism, stress, angst and pressure that they're getting from their manager.
6. A high degree of micro-management.
7. You're starting to feel very anxious the night before your work week starts, or physically sick at the thought of going to work.

The kind of culture a business has, generally filters down from the top. They set the scene and the example – good or bad. While I'm a big advocate of trying to influence something and you can certainly try to in this case, the reality is, it's unlikely you're going to be able to change a very negative culture on your own, unless you're the new head honcho. Find something else and get out before it starts to affect you too much.

74

Don't get into email bunfights

If you're emailing a colleague and the mood starts to get in any way annoyed, contentious or feathers are being ruffled, just stop. Don't get into a back-and-forth of increasingly snarky emails. It doesn't achieve anything useful and may well come back to bite you in the ass if a complaint is escalated, however informally.

Walk away from it for a few minutes, preferably longer, and only come back to it when you're calm and you've had a chance to think about it from both sides.

Nope, you're not there yet, leave it for longer.

Only then do you decide your next step. But whatever that is, make it calm, constructive and in no way antagonistic. And it's easier to resolve things in person or through a call than via email.

Don't put anything in writing that you couldn't fully stand over (with zero blushes) if it was forwarded to your manager or the business owner. It will save you from many a red-faced moment.

75

Feedback is your chance to become even more shit-hot

If you're getting constructive feedback about areas that could be improved, there's generally a reason for it (unless everyone around you agrees that your manager is a complete twit or worse, which does occasionally happen).

Assuming that's not the case here, be open to constructive feedback. Actually, don't just be open to it – ask for it, welcome it and make it work to your advantage. Don't be getting all defensive – you might as well write 'potential problem child' on your forehead. If you go straight into defensive and upset mode, you more than likely have some past-history-related personal triggers to work through. Deal with them if you can, otherwise feedback sessions are never going to be fun, for you or your manager. In fact, your manager will dread your performance reviews.

If you're open to feedback and make adjustments every time, you become more and more skilled and valuable to an employer. Any employer. Being open to feedback is the equivalent of writing

– 'easy to work with, wants to learn, this one could go far' on your forehead. What do you mean your forehead's too small to write that on?

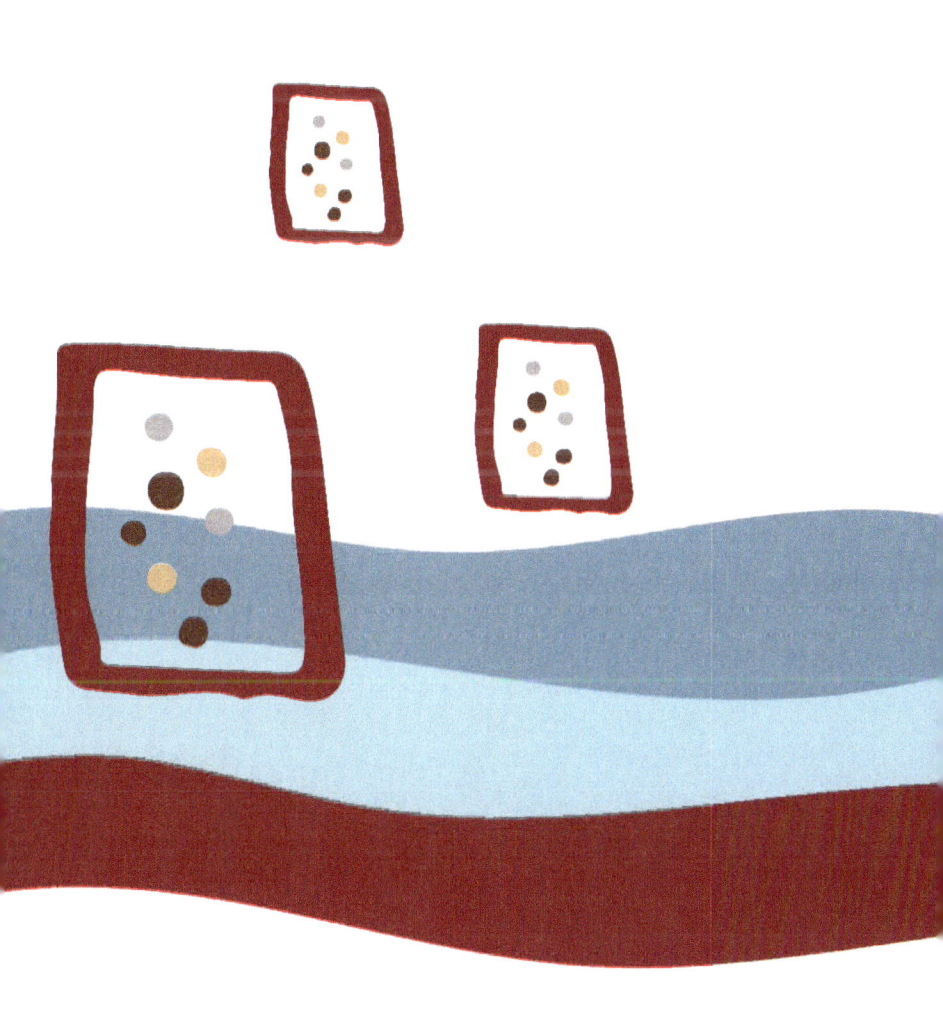

76

To find the best solution, you have to dig

You can't come up with a solution to a problem or challenge at work, until you fully understand the problem. There's a big difference between what you think or assume the problem is, or what one person tells you it is, and what is actually happening, the factors that are at play or even where the real problem lies. Dig, speak to multiple people and get the full picture first. Only then are you in a position to consider the best fix.

77

Protect your time like a mama bear protects her cub

Everyone's time is precious, including yours, and there are a lot of demands on it. So be careful with your time. Block out time in your calendar for your own work and to have some valuable thinking space.

You can always choose to free up a block here and there for important meetings, rather than having everyone else fill up your calendar. Some of these you will need to be at, some you won't, but you can decide.

If it's an update that's relevant to all of your team, it might be worth just one of the team attending, and then they can give the rest a summary briefing afterwards.

If someone has invited you and one of your teammates to a meeting, it may be that only one of you really needs to be there. If so, clarify that and free one of you up. The inviter may not have known who the right person to invite was, so they were hedging their bets.

And while we're on the topic of respecting your time and that of others, do not, do, not (not a typo), hit Reply All to emails, unless you're absolutely certain that everyone else simply has to know what your response is.

78

Sorry, I f@cked up

Admitting that you were wrong, made a mistake or messed up, is a sign of strength, maturity and ownership, not weakness. It's also generally appreciated. So put your hand up, so that things can be addressed, rectified or mitigated quickly, if needed.

If you did something that cost the company a lot of money or a client, put lives in danger or damaged their reputation, that's a different matter and may well cost you your job. But if you're being penalised or punished for a one-off honest mistake with relatively minor consequences, and a blame culture is the norm, then it may be time to look for a new work environment.

Mistakes happen. We all make them, and an employer with a mature and healthy work culture will be understanding and supportive. You can learn from it and move on.

79

Avoid your manager getting blindsided

I've never yet met a manager who liked to get unpleasant surprises, so it'll be much easier for you, and for them, to avoid them being blindsided or placed in an awkward situation with their peers or manager (unless you really don't like them and have a quick exit planned).

Forewarned is forearmed. It's part of having each other's back.

80

Staying on the right side of your manager

There are things you can do to have your manager eating out of your hand. AKA, know which side your bread is buttered on. And while you're at it, always keep on the right side of HR. (Unless you're a complete masochist, in which case go ahead and poke the bears.)

1. If there's something important or urgent that they've asked you to do, in fact anything that they seem anxious about – drop them a note to let them know as soon as it's done.
2. Ask if there's anything you can help with if they seem snowed under or just not themselves. Even if there's nothing you can do, the moral support will be appreciated.
3. Be proactive when it comes to picking things up and dealing with them without being asked to. Particularly if it takes something off their plate that you know they'd be comfortable with you handling.
4. Become a safe pair of hands that they can rely on, so they know that if they give you something to do, it will be done, on time and well.

5. If you ever flag a problem or challenge, always have ideas on how to address it, or even better, offer to look after it. Don't bring your manager more problems to solve.
6. Get along with your colleagues (you don't have to like them to work with them) and don't cause friction. I don't mean you should be a doormat. I mean be constructive, positive, helpful, supportive and a problem solver that can help keep the show on the road.
7. Listen to and be open to constructive feedback without getting defensive or taking it personally. It's your manager's job to give you feedback. If you can take it on board maturely and adapt, that will serve you well.
8. Take ownership of your career. Have thoughts around where you'd like to go, so that you can ask for your manager's support and advice on getting there. Then take the necessary steps to progress things.
9. Do your bit towards creating a good team dynamic and atmosphere. Help with organising nights out and team-building activities.

> In summary, be easy to work with. That sounds very trite, but I bet you can think of a few people at work who aren't. It doesn't mean that you can't challenge things constructively or push back. Sometimes that's exactly what's needed. What I'm saying is that work is hard enough for everyone as it is. So be pleasant, supportive and easy to work with. No one wants to spend eight hours or more a day with someone who isn't.

81

What's the 'So What'?

I had the privilege of having a wonderful mentor for a few years, the incredible Paula Covey. This question, along with 'How have we moved the dial?' was one of her trademark challenges to us.

You can write or say all sorts of things that you think your employees, customers or partners will want to hear, but none of it will be as strong or compelling as it could be, until you've applied that one simple test – what's the So What?

Imagine that you've just delivered a presentation. Your audience is sitting in front of you, listening, and once you've finished, they say, 'So what? Why should we care? Why are you taking up our valuable time with this?' (Sheesh. Tough audience, this.) What would you say to them?

Now go back to what you originally planned to say or write, in whatever kind of content you're creating. Is the 'So What?' covered? If it's not, include it before you finalise or deliver that content. When you apply the 'So What?', you tend to come up with the real gold. Suddenly, it gets a lot more powerful and meaningful.

82

Communications best practice

Whether or not you work in Communications, everyone needs to communicate, either internally or externally. And even if you're not the one creating business content, you might be giving input to it, approving it or delivering it.

I'm talking about everything from an email or internal announcement to a social post, customer communication, FAQ, brochure, annual report, web or video content.

Here are a few things to keep in mind:

1. Content needs to be created from the perspective of the audience that it's for. Imagine you're them and when you review it, ask yourself this: Do I find this relevant and useful? Does it include what I'd want to know? Is it interesting? Does it address my main concerns? Is there a clear takeaway? If I need to contact someone about this, are the contact details easy to find and use?

2. If you're trying to extract the most valuable content from a subject matter expert, focus on the best questions to ask them. If you do that, the right content should follow.
3. Consider what's happened in the past, which might or should influence how you approach this. Will there be concerns or sensitivities because of past events, in the market or in the company?
4. Don't include details that the audience doesn't need to know. People are busy; they appreciate brevity. If in doubt, feck it out.
5. Don't bring internal complexities to external audiences. Your business might be as complex as a spaghetti-like junction over a motorway, but keep things simple for customers.
6. Unless it's a specific type of technical or legal document, keep the language straightforward and informal. In general, write it the way you'd say it if you were explaining it to someone who didn't know your business.
7. Have you covered the What, Why, Who, Where, When and How, if all are relevant? And of all of those, often the most meaningful and engaging is the Why.
8. Is the order of content logical? I.e. does it tell people what this is about, why it's important, highlight any actions early on and finish with where they can find further info or what the next steps will be?
9. Anticipate the audience's likely questions, and either address them in the communication or be ready for them afterwards.
10. Does it pass the 'So what, why should I care?' test? I.e., does it include, in some form, the answer to that question if you imagine one of the audience asking you that?
11. Is it concise and easy to understand? Run it past someone in a different team and ask them.
12. When there's a design element sitting alongside written content, where is your eye drawn first? Design should complement the content; it shouldn't distract from it. The same applies to sound.

83

Enjoyable presentations (yes, they can actually be engaging)

Would you rather stick pins in your eyeballs (don't try that at home; do I even need to say this?) than sit through one or more hours of presentations at work? Is it hard to stay awake, particularly if it's warm? Presentations don't have to put people into a daydreaming trance. You can make them more interesting and entertaining. But it does take more time, effort and rehearsal time than just cobbling a few slides or thoughts together and talking them through.

If presenting to small or large groups of people is part of your role, the following tips may help:

1. When prepping what you want to say, it's about getting the relevant points and only the relevant points across in a way that they'll remember. So, keep it tight and concise. People will only remember two to three key takeaways anyway. What do they really need to know?

2. Include the facts or evidence that backs up the points you want to make. And make it clear why the audience should care about this topic (the 'So What') or what's in it for them.
3. Don't be predictable. Surprise them (in a good way), and they'll be more likely to pay attention because they won't know what you're going to do next. If you can do the presentation without any slides at all, brilliant, do that. Having some physical props, a short video or some images instead is a lot more interesting.
4. Grab their attention at the start. Begin with something interesting and unexpected, e.g. a personal fact about you (it can help to build a connection); a famous quote or surprising statistic about the topic you're about to talk about; a question for the audience, etc. Something that sets the scene for the main point you want to make.
5. Write out the full script of what you want to say and underline the key points. You'll need this for rehearsing it out loud. Ideally, memorise the script so you can focus on the delivery rather than reading from notes.
6. Build in some pauses, for example after you've just made a key point that you want them to digest for a moment. Don't be afraid of a few moments of silence. These can have a lot of impact. Look at some of the best political speakers or stand-up comedians and how well they employ moments of silence.
7. Rehearse, rehearse, rehearse and time yourself so you know the presentation will fit your allocated time.
8. If you do use slides, make them more visual (e.g. one simple image, a photo or graph) and not very wordy. Think three to four very concise bullet points per slide max, or one statement, quote or fact. What's on the slides should back up or complement what you're saying, they shouldn't *be* what you're saying. If you want people to switch off, show

them some slides packed full of small text and then start reading it all out.

9. Make it interactive and more of a two-way street rather than just you speaking to them. Use polls, ask them to put their hands up for some questions, ask them to get up and stretch (or attempt a complicated yoga pose) – whatever is unexpected but appropriate for that particular session and group of people.

10. Part of making it interactive is building eye contact and constantly reading the room. Read their expressions and actions and adapt accordingly. Interact with your audience and watch them respond to that.

11. Speak slowly, particularly if there are people in the group where your language is not their native tongue. It's much easier to follow and they'll be more likely to listen attentively, particularly when you include pauses, eye contact and the odd surprise.

12. Make a strong finish – do a recap of your key points, include a fact that reiterates why this topic is important. The more creative, the better. If there's an action they need to take, remind them then.

13. Don't let presentative time eat into Q&A time – because interaction is a critical part of the presentation.

84

Make summarising one of your superpowers

I worked with a creative agency once, and the Managing Director loved to quote Mark Twain. "I apologise for such a long letter – I didn't have time to write a short one."

The ability to summarise takes time and effort. It's harder to think through what the most pertinent details are, and only use them, but's a very valuable skill. Most people are busy and already inundated with information. It's coming at them from colleagues, friends and family, social media, the TV, news and radio. We have information overload fatigue. No one needs more unnecessary detail.

Make your emails, messages and updates concise. Not curt, just avoiding the unnecessary details. Cut to the chase. It will be appreciated. Plus, it shows you understand and can focus on the parts that your audience needs, and will be interested in.

85

Respect your experience

You're not 16 anymore (unless you are, in which case this is not aimed at you – go forth and enjoy your youth). You may still feel a little like a newbie or junior on the inside (even in your thirties or forties), but if you have a few years of experience under your belt, then you have skills. Respect that experience, and the next time you feel that you have something to say, to suggest or to flag, speak up.

Thinking that the other people in the room will surely have more experience, or better ideas and input than you? Not always the case.

Don't let imposter syndrome overshadow the reality of your knowledge, experience, achievements and successes. Because that was all you. Your employer and colleagues can benefit from that. Flex those muscles.

86

Work is the most important thing in your life

No, it's not. Just seeing if you were paying attention there after your initial a) nodding head or b) mild outrage at seeing that heading.

Work is definitely important when it comes to being able to pay the bills and buy things, like food (very important, fair enough). And it's important to have a role and a purpose, as fulfilling as you can make it. But. Your health and your relationships with loved ones are more important. So don't risk either of them for a job. You can always get another job.

87

Making career moves

So, you want to progress, get more experience, get promoted and develop your career. Great. Let's look at a few contextual, background elements that will influence the outcome and then the things that you can do to help make things happen.

The background landscape

Your current employer is more likely to be open to giving a promotion when:
1. They can see how it will help them achieve sales targets, strategic goals or meet customer demands. And there's no one currently doing that role at that level, or not enough people doing it.
2. The business believes it can afford the additional salary and benefits associated with that promotion.
3. A vacancy has just arisen because someone left and it's a back-fill rather than an additional headcount (and cost).

Some myths about promotion

Most companies won't promote you simply due to time served, even if you have a consistently good performance record. There's usually more to it than that, including whether there's a business need for a person in that role, at that level. And it's not your manager's responsibility to promote you. They definitely have a role to play here to support you, but the person who needs to drive your career and make changes happen is you. And you can make that happen.

Things you can do to help get promoted

1. Be clear about what you want. Is it the next grade up in your current role or experience in a different role or team? Do you want to be a technical expert? Do you want to manage people or not? If you're not sure what you want to do, speak to a career advisor, your HR team, a mentor or do some aptitude tests to see which roles would suit your personality and strengths.
2. Once you know what you want and where you want to go, discuss it with your manager at performance review time (or before) so they're aware, and can advise and support you.
3. Make use of any development tools or courses available to you at work, which support your plan and build your skills and knowledge. Then demonstrate those skills.
4. Network and build useful contacts. Speak to people within the business who currently do the role that you're interested in. Let the manager of that team know that you're interested in upcoming opportunities.
5. Offer to support someone currently doing that role, outside of your normal hours, to gain experience. It takes time and effort but it shows you're really serious about the move.

See how you feel about it after getting some insights into the reality of the role. You may like it even more, or less.

6. There may be an opportunity to do a temporary job shadow or become involved in a cross-functional project.

7. Build your profile. Be an active participant in meetings and calls. Speak up. Show you're engaged. Ask questions, give your ideas and views. Take opportunities to showcase the results of your work.

8. Bring well-thought-through ideas that you think will benefit the team, the business, your customers or partners, to your manager.

9. We all have bad days, but be as consistently positive, constructive, responsive, solution-oriented, flexible and supportive as you can. That's the mindset that others enjoy working with the most and want in their team.

10. Demonstrate that you're a safe and reliable pair of hands to give more challenging or complex tasks to, even if it's a topic that doesn't particularly interest you. Volunteer for things – it is noticed. Some tasks are fun and interesting, some are tedious, but they all still need to be done.

11. If you see and are interested in a vacancy, let your manager know and apply for it. Don't wait to be approached or encouraged. Go for it. The very act of applying for something says you're serious about it, even if you don't get it the first time.

You have choices

If you're looking for a promotion but it isn't happening at the moment, you can:

1. Take a wait-and-see approach, if you'd rather stay in your existing team but there are no new roles coming up to apply for yet. Invest in self-development and up-skill in the meantime. Work out how much time you're prepared to give it, before trying a different tack.

2. Is there the potential to up-skill and create a brand-new role that the business needs to fulfil a strategic goal or target? Demonstrate how you can help the company achieve that. Become their 'go-to' person for that topic. If a role is created, you'll be in a much stronger position to get it.
3. Weigh up what's most important to you. The pros and cons of staying where you are or looking for another opportunity. Different people value different things. Salary, title, relationships with existing co-workers, job security, pension and benefits, the level of challenge and variety in a role, the need for change and whether you're still learning (or not). That will shape your actions.
4. And if it just isn't happening, despite your efforts, and the deadline that you set for yourself is up, you can always look for a role in another team in the same company, in a completely different company, or go self-employed.

88

Embrace change (or, my preferred title, Be the Polo Pony)

From what I've seen, resisting change at work is the default, most common reaction. Whether the business you work for has been acquired, you're re-branding, your employer is merging with another company or your manager is making major changes within the team. It will be a lot less stressful for you if you can adjust internally to embrace that change rather than fighting it all the way.

If you have a good reason for resisting something, e.g. you believe it will damage the business's reputation or make things worse for customers or partners, then by all means speak up and fight your corner.

But if the main reason you're resisting change, if you're honest with yourself, is because you prefer to stick with what you're familiar with, they're changing something you set up (your baby), or the change is just plain uncomfortable, try and let it go. It's time for change and your baby might just be becoming a toddler.

Don't make it harder on yourself than it needs to be. These changes are more than likely going to happen anyway. So you can choose to go there willingly, engage, and influence the hell out of it, or you can take the longer, harder and more stressful road.

Are you going to be a slow-moving, stubborn mule or a nippy polo pony who gets in the game, moves quickly and helps to shape the changes?

If you take the polo pony approach, you have a better chance of snaffling one of the nicer stables and some of the tastier food at the new ranch. Food for thought?

89

When you're on holiday, be on holiday

None of this checking emails and taking work calls. That's not a holiday and it's not sustainable. You need complete breaks from work from time to time, to be at your best, most productive and creative when you are at work.

I know that's easier said than done when you work for yourself, are in a team of one or when you're in a job where you're regularly on call for emergencies. But do what you can to get a proper break, and to reduce the avalanche of work waiting for you when you get back, which negates the benefits of a holiday.

If you're part of a team, agree how it will work so that you can cover for each other when one of you is on leave. Then, whoever's about to go on leave – do a handover email for the others so they know what might come up, what needs to be progressed and where documents that they might need are filed. This is part of having each other's back and supporting each other within a team.

Set your email out-of-office, letting people know who to go to for what (if you're in a team), when you'll be back, and do something similar for your work phone voice mail.

A good employer or manager won't ask you to work on your holidays unless there's some kind of major emergency or exceptional situation.

90

Be careful around Them and Us thinking

I'm talking about different teams and departments in the same company or group. When there are some frustrations, it can be easy to fall into 'them and us' type thinking, where you're making all sorts of assumptions about another team, not always flattering. It can get a little tribal and it never achieves anything constructive.

You're all in the same company and on the same team as far as your customers are concerned. You all want the business to be successful, because it's paying you and helping you to pay your bills.

Rather than digging your mental trenches, you need to increase collaboration and understanding of the pressures, challenges, priorities and thought processes of the other team(s). Get a rep from the other team in to talk at one of your team meetings and reciprocate. Get around a table and be honest and up front about any frustrations you're experiencing, and listen to their feedback and frustrations, so that you can find a way to work together more smoothly going forward.

91

Stop and lift your head up from the never-ending prairie that is your task list

You're adding value by getting on with those day-to-day tasks but you can add a lot more. We tend to get into a rhythm of familiar activity and keep doing that, rather than zooming out to look at what's happening and adapting when needed.

Take a few moments, an hour, a few times a year to just stop and take stock. Think about the business and what's happening with it recently, with your role, your team, your customers and what's happening in the market and wider world. For example:

1. Is there something happening in the market, or about to happen, that customers, or employees, need to be reassured about?

2. Has the business changed or grown to the extent where some current processes or team structures are no longer fit for purpose?
3. Are there new innovations or software that you could harness, to make life easier for your customers or help employees do their job?
4. What seems to be working well within the business, the team or with customers, that you can do more of, and what's not working well or causing frustration?
5. What does the business need to be or do, to keep up with or go beyond customers' changing expectations?
6. What are customers, suppliers, partners or employees saying that you really need to pay attention to and act on?
7. What challenges or opportunities can you see coming down the track that you can do something about now?
8. What topics are customers most interested in right now that you could provide useful information about?

Based on that kind of assessment, what's most important and needed today? If it's all being addressed, great. If not, what are the action areas?

Thinking about things like this, beyond the day-to-day, raising these topics with your colleagues and choosing which ones to act on – that's where you can add value above and beyond. Stop munching on that grass and look up and around you.

92

Walking the managerial seesaw

Part of being a manager is constantly trying to find a middle ground between two things. On one side you have what your team wants – their preferences, perspectives and what works best for them. On the other side you have what the business needs from your team and what's in the business's best interests.

If you tip the balance too far towards one of those sides, things will start to suffer on the other. For example – the dates that people in the team want to take their holidays on, versus the business's busy periods when you need to have enough cover for certain functions. Or a business's targets around training hours per year, versus your team's time for training and up-skilling alongside their typical workload.

You're regularly making decisions that try to keep both sides of that seesaw as happy as possible. Being able to do that will involve some very honest and up-front conversations at times.

93

Interview tips for managers

It's not just about finding the right person for the job. It's about making sure they'll fit with the culture, be happy and work well with you and the rest of your team. You'll want to avoid hiring someone who's the wrong fit and having to go through the process all over again.

Pre-interview

You'll have whittled down the CVs to the most promising ones. Aim to interview six to eight people for a role, with the aim of having three to four to choose from at the final stage. You need to allow for some drop-outs, as some candidates may accept a job offer elsewhere during your interview process.

The initial contact to arrange that first-round meeting is part of the interview process and assessment:

1. Are they easy to deal with and reasonably flexible when it comes to setting an interview date and time that works for them and for you?

2. Do they seem keen to have the interview?
3. If they're late for an interview or need to reschedule, that could be for perfectly legitimate reasons (and works both ways), but if it happens regularly for a two- to three-stage interview, it may be a red flag.

During the interview(s)

After the greetings and initial polite small talk to put the person at ease (I think you get the best insights into people when they're feeling relaxed rather than nervous), the following are useful questions to choose from to ask the interviewee. You could split them over a couple of interviews:

1. Would you summarise your qualifications and experience to date please? (AKA, are you able to be concise and does what you say match what you sent us?)
2. What do you currently know about [company name]? (AKA, are you genuinely interested in this business?)
3. What attracted you to this particular role? (Similar goal to Question 2.)
4. What would you describe as the strongest single attribute that you bring to an employer?
5. What would you say is your greatest weakness or area for development? (AKA, how self-aware are you, how much are you going to divulge here and how well do you deal with tricky questions?)
6. Where do you see yourself in five years' time and how do you see this role helping you to get there? (AKA, do you have an idea of how you'd like your career to develop?)
7. How would you approach your first three months if you were offered the role? (AKA how proactive are you and how would you go about finding out what's most important in the role?)

8. How would you describe your ideal manager? (AKA, what management style do you respond to best?)
9. What motivates you the most at work?
10. Can you give me an example of something that frustrated you at work and how you dealt with it? (AKA, give me an insight into how you deal with workplace challenges, how diplomatic you are and how well you work with others.)
11. Why do you wish to leave your current role? (AKA, is this about taking the next step in your career or is there something else happening that I should know about?)
12. Can you tell me about any innovations, fresh ideas or process improvements you brought to your last role or team?
13. What was your impression of our [social channels/website/products] and is there anything you think we could improve on? (AKA, did you spot things that could be better, because that would be useful to hear, and do you have the confidence to mention them?)
14. Did you have any questions for me/us? (AKA, wow me with your insights, curiosity and show me just how engaged you are in this process.)
15. Now that we've spoken more, are you still interested in the role? (AKA, do you still want this, to avoid wasting your time and my time in any further interview steps?)
16. Do you have any other first-, second- or third-round interviews or job offers at the moment? (AKA, if I want to hire you, how much time do I have to make a decision or do I need to act quickly?)
17. If you were successful in this recruitment process, when would you be available to start?

Post-interview

Once the interview rounds are over, you'll hopefully have three or four candidates to choose from before you approach one with an offer. Who can you most easily envisage in the role and who do you most want to hire? Know your number one and two choices, just in case your first choice drops out.

If you have some doubts or reservations about any of those candidates, even if you can't quite put your finger on what it is, listen to them. What is your gut saying? Always go with your gut.

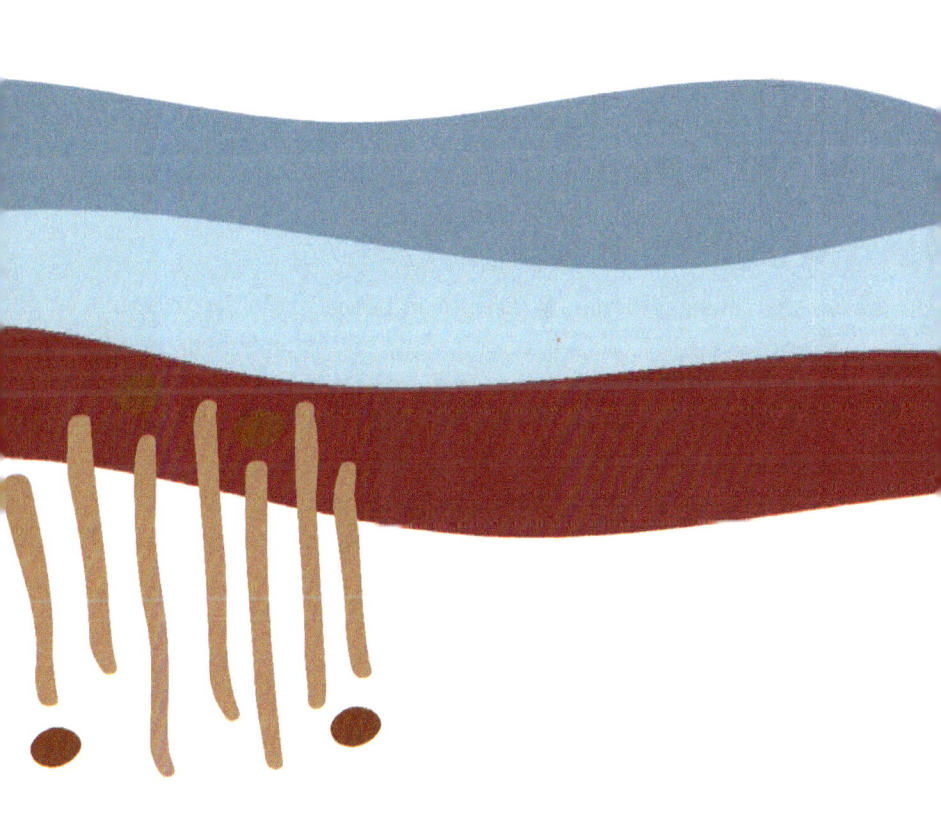

94

Ruling through fear or trust

I've seen managers rule by fear. It can be very effective in terms of results, but it's also a very unhealthy, unsustainable approach that will backfire over time, due to employee turnover or absenteeism among other things. Plus, it places unnecessary stress on people. You'll never get as much from your team and you won't get the benefit of their full potential. They'll be too afraid to be at their most proactive or creative or to give useful feedback on what improvements could be made.

Far better to lead by being authentic, empathetic, showing some vulnerabilities, taking a firm but fair approach and nurturing two-way trust. If things get tough in the business or market and everyone needs to pull together to survive, that team dynamic is much more likely to get through it and come out stronger on the other side.

95

Staying on the right side of your team

If you're managing a team, here are a few things to keep in mind for a happy (as much as people can be at work, it's still work), motivated and productive team. These are part of your role as a manager:

1. Ask them how they are, regularly, and mean it. Listen to what they say and how they respond to the question.
2. In the same vein, occasionally ask how their partner, children (or even their pets) are, particularly if one of them is sick. After all, you hired a whole person and they come with a whole life.
3. Notice when they're behaving out of character and check in with them to make sure they're okay.
4. Share something personal about your life outside of work that you're comfortable with sharing. Interests, hobbies, things you feel passionate about. It creates a better relationship when you can share more of your whole self.

5. Be firm but fair, honest and direct and set clear boundaries. Explain what you expect of them, in the role and team, including their key deliverables for that year.
6. Be clear on what decisions they're allowed or not allowed to make, so they know the boundaries of the role and can feel more autonomous. That might be around what budget threshold they can authorise or business decisions they can make.
7. Take the time to give them feedback. On the great stuff that they're doing at least as much as any constructive feedback on things to improve.
8. Ask what their career aspirations are and give them advice and support in getting there.
9. Give them opportunities to increase their profile within the business. Showcase their work and make sure they get the kudos for it.
10. Say Thank You and tell them the things that impressed you, that you really appreciated, or if they did something that made your job easier. Don't just think that stuff. Say it.
11. Notice when they're stagnating in their role and are ready for new, interesting challenges and help them to stretch into that.
12. Stand up for them, and with them, when needed. And fight for team resources when required.
13. Help them gain the confidence to do more, speak up more and make greater use of their experience.
14. Don't let destructive or negative behaviour within the team go unaddressed.
15. Don't micromanage – this is a big one. Being more prescriptive with new starters or someone who's just getting to grips with a more senior role is one thing. If they're experienced and capable in their role, let them get on with it and just be there if they want a second opinion. They may not do things exactly the way you would. That's okay.

In summary, be real, firm but fair, be honest, care about your team, go the extra mile for them, have their back and you'll often create a culture where they'll look after you the same way. It can create one hell of a team. One that can survive the ups and downs of work life. And you'll have a better chance of keeping those skills and experience within the team or business.

96

It takes two to find a resolution

You may be applying all the best practice that you can, but at some point, as a manager, you're likely to experience a challenging situation with one of your team. The challenge might be behavioural, poor performance, a rigid mindset, unrealistic demands or causing problems with customers, partners, suppliers or teammates.

You'll feel it's your responsibility as the manager to sort this out, to talk to them, support them, and help everyone get past this. And you're right. You should try and address this. You'll need to listen, and they'll need to listen.

There's a good chance you'll be able to sort out the majority of situations like this. But you will not win them all and you need to know when to stop pouring energy into it.

You can do your very best, but if things aren't improving, if there's a blind spot they just can't get past, there comes a point where you need to step back. Too much time or energy spent on one person is taking time away from other members of the team. Receptivity to feedback and resolving things needs to come equally from both parties. That won't always happen. Know when to stop.

Finances

97

Start a pension as soon as you start working

Even if retirement seems far away right now, starting a pension is one of the most important financial decisions you'll ever make, for one of the biggest potential benefits. Why do you need one? The pension you'll get from the state will definitely help, but in many countries it won't stretch much beyond food and utilities, and that's if you're lucky. It probably won't come close to the income you had when you were working. So, you're going to need something to top-up that state pension when you retire.

Think of a pension as being like having your own personal money tree. The sooner you plant that little acorn and keep feeding it, the longer it has to grow, slowly and quietly, in the background of your life. If you're in your twenties now, brilliant. You have the opportunity to make time work hard for you. The longer that tree has to get bigger, the more money you can harvest from it. Even if you're older than your twenties, start paying into a pension as soon as you can.

Pensions are generally tax efficient, one of the big benefits over traditional savings plans.

If you're working for a company that offers a pension plan, they'll typically pay an amount into it for you every month. But put something towards it yourself every month too (if your contribution is optional rather than mandatory), even if it's only a small amount to start with, and increase it slowly each year.

If you're not working for a company that offers a pension plan, you can start your own private pension. Start with what you can afford to put in every month and then increase it over time.

What's happening in the financial markets can mean that the value of pensions goes up and down over time, but even if they take a knock, they can usually recover. The returns on pensions may not be iron-clad, but they're still typically a good idea and a good investment.

Plant that acorn. Your retired self will thank you.

98

It pays to make the big switch

In some cases, being a loyal customer just doesn't benefit you, in fact it's costing you money. This is typically the case when it comes to utilities – your electricity or gas supplier, TV package, streaming service, broadband and mobile phone supplier, etc. It pays to switch suppliers every year or as soon as you're outside your current contracted period. The same applies to your house, car and pet insurance.

Change suppliers and reap the discounts, rates or offers they're putting out there to attract new customers. It takes a little time and effort to switch, but it can save you hundreds per year.

So, shop around. There are also aggregator websites that make it very easy to switch utility and insurance providers, and they'll handle a lot of the administration for you, e.g. in Ireland there's Bonkers, Switcher, 123 or Chill. Check out the aggregators in your country.

99

Do I still want this?

If you're feeling flahoolick or just won the lottery, fine, but otherwise... When you find something you like but don't need, you can always choose to walk away from it for a while. Distract yourself and go and do something else.

If you still really want it an hour, a few hours or even a few days later, you can make a call on it then. But if you'd forgotten about it or don't feel such a strong desire to buy it now, that'll make it much easier to just leave it. The 'walk away for now' approach helps reduce spending, whether that's through impulse purchases, boredom or comfort shopping. As well as reducing your general accumulation of more stuff.

100

Savings first

Everyone experiences unexpected costs and income isn't always a reliable, certain thing. It pays to have a fund for emergencies, and you may be saving for something big.

Set up a savings account and a current account. As soon as you get paid, transfer the amount you want to save into your savings account. You can always set up a standing order from your current account to your savings account so you don't have to remember to make that transfer.

What's left in your current account is then your budget to live on, to cover your bills and discretionary spend until the next pay day.

Don't live on what's in your current account, and then see if there happens to be anything left at the end of the month that can be moved to your savings. Savings before Spends.

101

Pay off the most expensive debt first

Between credit cards and other loans, they'll all have an APR – an annual percentage rate. It's the interest rate you're charged on the loaned money, plus any additional fees or costs.

If you pay off your credit card in full and on time each month, you won't typically pay any interest on that money.

If you have other loans where you are paying interest, and you're in a position to start paying some of them off, like a student loan, car loan or other credit cards – tackle them one at a time. Start with the one with the highest APR. Once that's paid off, turn your attention to the debt with the next highest APR, and so on.

If debt feels overwhelming, call your local Citizens Advice Bureau or equivalent for free financial advice. And if you're having problems making your mortgage payments, call the bank and speak to them. Banks always prefer to know there's a problem and find a solution with you, such as lower payments for a period of time. Talking to them will generally get a better result for you than saying nothing and being late with payments.

102

Sometimes it's safer to ditch the credit card

If you really need to take control of your spending and not spend any more than you have coming in, consider ditching the credit card(s). Stick with your debit card for all day-to-day expenses.

103

Make a Will, please

As soon as you have any assets, if you own a car, bought a house, own land, livestock or shares, etc., you should make a Will. We all pop our clogs at some stage (unless you're a vampire or have a very scary painting of yourself in the attic). It's not being morbid, it's being pragmatic. You don't *have* to have a Will, but not having one can cause a lot of problems.

My dad was a farmer. Growing up, I regularly heard stories about families who were no longer speaking to each other because of disputes over land because the owner hadn't left a Will. This doesn't just apply to people who have a few fields.

If you don't have a Will, state inheritance laws kick in and your preferences won't be a factor. Distant relatives who never even met you could potentially get your assets, rather than the person or people you actually wanted to leave them to.

So if you want to have a say in who gets what, make a Will. Don't let disputes and divided families be your legacy. And don't think that explaining things verbally ten years ago will be enough. Things are forgotten or remembered differently over the years.

Making a Will is fairly quick and easy to do and it makes things easier and clearer for your remaining family. It can also state who you'd like your children's guardians to be, should anything happen.

Beforehand:

Check out the inheritance tax law in your country. You can usually find this online. Typically, there will be different thresholds of how much you can leave, tax-free, to relatives and friends, which is good to be aware of. If there are significant assets, you'll probably get specialist tax advice.

If you have children, speak to them, or whoever you plan to leave things to, and find out which of them are happy to be executors of your Will. These are the people who will execute the wishes expressed and make sure things are divvied up the way you want. Executors can be one or more of your children, other trusted relatives or friends. Having more than one executor can help spread the load of things that need to be done, so it's not all on one person's shoulders.

Making the Will:

1. Make an appointment with a solicitor or attorney (different names are used in different countries – I'll just say legal advisor from here on in).
2. Explain how you want to leave things and your legal advisor will help you craft the Will and advise you on anything you need to be aware of.
3. State who your executors will be.
4. A Will has to be witnessed and signed by other people. Your legal advisor will help with that.
5. If you have some smaller items of sentimental value, e.g. you want to leave your watch to a grandchild, those things can go into a separate document called Bequests, which doesn't need to be witnessed. What you have in it may change over time and you can simply email an updated copy to your legal advisor.

You can create your own will, but if you want to be certain it's legally valid, I'd recommend you go to a legal professional.

After getting your Will:

1. Don't ever staple or paperclip anything to it, as that can invalidate it.
2. Talk things through with your executor(s) so they have a chance to ask questions about the future administration of your Will and funeral wishes while you're still around. Let them know where your Will is stored, whether that's at your legal advisor's office (give the contact details) or in your home (say where).
3. Keep a copy of your list of Bequests (if you have one, it's not obligatory) with your Will (not stapled or paperclipped together), along with notes on whether you want to be buried or cremated, etc.
4. If you're keeping the original Will or copies of it in your home, store them in a fireproof bag. These are easy to buy on Amazon.
5. If you get married, divorced, have children or adopt children, update your Will.

104

Enduring power of attorney

Okay, I'm sorry. I probably shouldn't have put this straight after the section on Wills. You're nearly there (on the tough topics – bear with me).

If something happens to you, such as an illness or accident, and you're no longer able to make decisions and look after your financial and personal affairs, having an enduring power of attorney already in place means that you have someone (or more than one person) you trust who is legally authorised to step in and make those decisions on your behalf. They become your attorney(s).

The attorney doesn't make decisions about your medical treatment. You can state in advance what you want, and don't want, in the event that something happens to you.

A little like making a Will, having this in place, even if you're in great health, makes practical good sense, and makes things easier for you and your loved ones, if something does happen.

Rules around enduring power of attorney may differ from country to country but your local equivalent of a Citizens Advice Bureau will be able to advise you on how to go about setting this up.

Home

105

Have a backup plan for getting into your home

Give a spare key to a trusted friend or neighbour, attached to a large and colourful keyring (the larger and wackier, the better), so it's easy for them to find for you, if needed. These things are generally put in a drawer and forgotten about.

You never know, for any number of reasons, when you might suddenly find yourself without a key to get into your own home.

106

If there isn't a contract, clarify the details in writing

If you're planning to get a patio, your driveway paved or add a garden room, the details aren't always confirmed in a contract, because not all small companies issue contracts. You'll discuss the details with them verbally, but there may be assumptions being made on both sides. For expensive items or services where there isn't a contract, you can avoid a lot of potential problems by confirming the details in writing before the work starts.

Email the details to the supplier, based on the conversations you've had, and ask them to reply by email confirming that what you've written is correct, or clarifying anything that isn't. This is an example email to a supplier for a patio. You can adapt it to your situation.

Hi [name of your supplier contact],

Before the work on the [patio] is done, would you look over the information below and let me know if anything isn't correct please?

1. Client: [your name and telephone number].
2. Patio being added at: [your address].
3. Date of the job is [the date and duration you agreed with them], and I understand that bad weather may cause a delay.
4. Products: [the paving product name, colour, tile dimensions and total square footage needed, and the company it's being sourced from. Do the same for any kerbing, decking etc].
5. Design, layout and location of the patio [has been provided/will be provided by xx date].
6. The garden slopes upwards towards the back of the lawn. You've confirmed that you'll put in a step to address this.
7. You've confirmed that the work is guaranteed for [x] years, for paving cracks, subsidence, paving/kerbing not staying in place.
8. Will the areas not covered by paving be made ready for planting or is this something I need to look after?
9. After hardcore and other materials have been delivered and used, your team will make sure the road and driveway will be cleaned at the end of the job.
10. You've confirmed that you will deliver the paving and kerbing to my address.
11. Please confirm if payment is in instalments or all at the end of the job and which payment methods you accept.
12. Please confirm if the price breakdown below is correct [add the details you've been given for materials, labour, any extras you asked for, and VAT, with a final total figure].

107

Easy-access kitchen storage

To make the most of your kitchen storage space, and make it easier to find the items you want without having to take lots of other things out first:

1. To access non-perishable food in kitchen cabinets, get a few clear plastic, open-top storage boxes, about 10-15cm high, which fit the size and depth of your cupboards. You can just pull them out slightly to see what's in there and get at the things stored at the very back of the box. These are also useful for storing cleaning products under the sink.
2. If you use spices and herbs in your cooking, buying a spice carousel makes it easy to lay your hands on the bottle you want without having to take lots of small bottles out of the cabinet first, and then put them all back in.
3. Getting a horizontal, expandable pan-organiser rack is great for storing frying pans, saucepans and lids on their sides. You can adjust the wire spacers so they fit the size of your pans and lids. It's much easier to just grab the one you want, rather than having to lift off other things first and

then put them all back in. There are also vertical racks if that suits your cupboard space better.

108

Ditch the five-year-old tinned food (your home isn't an underground World War II bunker)

Once every couple of years, have a clear-out of your kitchen's food cupboards. If you haven't done this for a while, you get to feel slightly sheepish about the food that's five, seven or ten years or more out of date (that can't just be me). *That's* where that jar of redcurrant jelly got to.

Compost everything that's out of date. And just look at all that space you have now, which will be filled up in a matter of days, because nature abhors an empty cupboard.

109

Getting the most from your freezer

I have a friend who told me once that she'd never seen anyone use a freezer as much as I did. I thought at the time, *What? Doesn't everybody?* (Mum, the apple doesn't fall far from the tree.)

To avoid having to throw things out that you haven't had a chance to eat before they've gone past their use-by date, remember that you can freeze the following common items (among other things):

1. Bread
2. Cheese (blocks or bags of grated cheese)
3. Milk (let it defrost slowly)
4. Butter

You can then pluck them out of the freezer at a later date with a flourish, when you're hungry and just can't be arsed going to the supermarket.

Let things cool properly before freezing. Freeze in one- or two-portion quantities, e.g. four sausages, two slices of bread, etc., so you can just take out what you need, as you need it. Use air-tight rigid plastic or glass containers, re-usable silicone bags or zip-top freezer bags.

Remember to double-wrap raw meat well, smoothing out any air (and write the date on a label) before freezing to reduce the chance of freezer burn (if that happens, the food will look wrinkly and taste weird). I use a compostable greaseproof paper to wrap the meat, then put it in a re-usable silicone food bag.

Every couple of months, have an 'eating out of the freezer' week, where you use up whatever's in there, starting with the older items first.

110

The all-round, do-everything kitchen knife

I'm talking about the Victorinox tomato knife. I have more of these in my cutlery drawer than you could shake a stick at. They may have been designed for chopping tomatoes but I use them for pretty much everything. As a general dinner or steak knife, for chopping vegetables, fruit, small loaves of bread, as well as tomatoes. They're regular dinner knife-sized, lightweight and super sharp.

111

Hand-wash non-stick cookware

Non-stick saucepans, frying pans, baking trays, roasting dishes and air fryer drawers – yes, you can put many of them in the dishwasher, but hand-washing non-stick items will help them last a lot longer.

112

Towels gone as rough as a badger's bum?

If your towels have gone from soft and fluffy, to feeling like scratchy cardboard, and you'd like to get them soft again:

1. Put them in your washing machine with half a mug of vinegar (in the washing liquid/powder compartment). No washing liquid or fabric softener. Don't over-stuff the washing machine as the towels will need space to move around.
2. Wash them at the temperature recommended on the towel's label. I generally use 40 degrees. Only wash them, no drying cycle.
3. When that wash cycle is finished, add a heaped tablespoon of baking powder on top of the wet towels. Again, no washing liquid or fabric softener.
4. Wash them again at the same temperature as before.
5. Then tumble dry.
6. Done.

113

Getting blood stains out of clothes

If you cut your finger chopping veg in the kitchen and managed to get blood on your white T-shirt (or however it happened – hopefully we're not talking crime scene here), get the item into cold water as soon as you can. Hold it under the cold tap for a while to flush the stain out and then hand-wash it in cold water with some soap.

If that got the stain out completely, great, you can put it in the washing machine as part of a bigger load and wash as normal at a warm temperature.

If it didn't, you can pour some salt onto the stain while the material is still wet from its cold hand-wash, and use a little cold water to make a paste. Leave that on the stain for 15-20 mins, rinse out and then wash at a warm temperature as normal.

114

When pillowcases go rogue

If you've ever gone to change the sheets on a bed and found that one of the pillowcases from the set has gone AWOL, this one's for you.

Once you've washed and dried the duvet cover and pillowcase(s), fold up your duvet cover and one of the pillowcases (if it's a double/king set) and pop them both into the second pillowcase, so it acts like a storage bag. Easiest way to keep everything together.

115

Getting rid of water marks on wooden furniture

If drink glasses have left ring-shaped water marks on your unvarnished wooden furniture, rub some clear Vaseline or Lypsyl into the water marks and they should disappear or at least become less noticeable.

116

The great Anti-Squeak

Ah, the wonder-oil that is WD-40.

Just spray some on the hinges of squeaky doors. Open and close the door a few times to work the oil into the hinge. Also works for squeaky mechanisms in office chairs and helps metal zippers run more smoothly.

You can spray it onto the metal parts of garden tools and then wipe them down to help keep them rust-free.

It's also great for the runner wheels at the top and bottom of sliding shower doors. Spray them three to four times a year to keep the wheels moving freely.

117

Bleeding radiators

When I moved out of my parents' house into my first home, I'd heard about bleeding radiators but had no idea what that meant or what I needed to do. If your home's heating system runs warm water through radiators, then they'll need to be bled once a year. Otherwise, over time, air can get trapped in the system, stopping the hot water from reaching all parts of the radiator.

You'll know the radiator needs to be bled when the bottom of it is warm, but the top is cold, even when your heating is running.

This is what you need to do:

1. You'll need the radiator key. Often this is stored on top of the radiator or close by. It's just a small plastic or metal tool that opens the bleed valve. You'll generally find the bleed valve near the top, on one side of the radiator.
2. If you don't have the radiator key, take a photo of the bleed valve, a note of its dimensions, and you should be able to buy a key that fits it in a hardware store.
3. Turn off your heating system, just while you bleed the radiators.

4. Get an old towel and a cloth. Put the towel on the floor underneath the valve.
5. Hold the key in the cloth and slowly open the bleed valve. Continue to open it very gradually until you can hear the hiss of air escaping. Don't open the valve any further at this stage.
6. Once all the air has escaped, some water will start to come out of the valve. You have the towel below you just in case. Tighten the valve back up at that stage.
7. Repeat with the other radiators.
8. Turn your heating back on and your radiators should all be heating up properly, top and bottom.

And if that doesn't solve the problem, you may need to call in your local friendly plumber.

118

Maximising wardrobe space

If you're running out of space for your clothes and you've already had a clear-out of anything that hasn't been worn in months or years, or no longer fits, vacuum storage bags can help. Once you've placed your clothes in, you can use the small hand pump that came with the vacuum bag (or a vacuum cleaner) to take the air out and shrink the bag down so it's taking up minimal space.

Your warmer season clothes can go into storage in some of these bags as you start coming into the colder seasons. And you can then swap them out for your colder season clothes when the weather warms up. Store the bags in an attic, wardrobe or under your bed.

Replace thick wooden or plastic hangers with slimline velvet ones. They not only take up much less space in your wardrobe, but your clothes won't slide off them either.

Use open-fronted shoe boxes in the bottom of your wardrobe, so you can stack them and store two layers of shoes in the space between the bottom of hanging clothes and the base of your wardrobe.

119

The big mattress flip

It's easy to forget about your mattress. It's just there, covered in sheets, duvet and pillows. A quiet workhorse, like your favourite armchair or sofa. Next thing you know, it's 12 or more years old, at which point you get a new one and think, *Oh, pocket spring or memory foam bliss. Why didn't I do this sooner?*

Generally, you should be aiming to replace your mattress every eight years.

120

House plants that are generally hard to kill

Two of the easiest houseplants to look after (and not kill through too much or too little watering or light) that I've ever found are:

1. The parlour palm (*Chamaedorea elegans*). It is, as per its name, an elegant arching plant that will eventually give you some nice tall greenery in a room, depending on how old it is.
2. The ZZ plant (*Zamioculcas zamiifolia*). A great-looking plant (it's so healthy-looking it looks artificial) that's particularly useful for rooms with low levels of natural light. Just be careful if you have children or pets as the leaves and sap are toxic if eaten. Wear gloves if you're pruning it.

121

Setting a hearth fire

If you move into a house with an open fireplace, and the previous owner confirmed that it's safe to use, then great. Otherwise, it's probably best to get the fireplace and chimney checked and cleaned by a professional before using it.

When it's been given the all-clear, here's how to set a fire:

1. Use the poker (from the fireside set of tools) and move it back and forth across the top of the grate at the bottom of the fireplace, to knock any ash down through the gaps in the grate. I prefer the poker to the brush for this as sometimes ash can still have warm embers from the night before.
2. If the space below the grate is full of ash, use the small spade to shovel it out and dispose of it. Your fire won't get going properly if this space is full of ash.
3. Once the ash has been cleared from above and below the grate, find an old newspaper, tear double-spread sheets out and crumple each of them into fairly tight paper balls.
4. Put a layer of the crumpled paper balls on top of the grate, packing them in relatively tightly.

5. You'll then need some kindling (bought or made) – thin slivers of dry wood. Put one layer of kindling on top of the paper, pointing slightly left, leaving a little space in between each of them. Do the same with another layer of kindling on top of the first, pointing slightly right, so the wood is criss-crossing like a lattice.
6. If you have some, you can place four to six lumps of smokeless coal on top of the kindling, again, leaving some space between each piece. Leave this step out if you don't have smokeless coal, and for a more sustainable option.
7. Light the paper layer in two or three places at the front of the fireplace. Once it catches well and all of the kindling is burning, you can start to very gradually feed in more wood (start with the smallest logs). When it's all burning well and the fire is more established, you can add in one or two larger logs.
8. Stand the fire guard up in front of the grate as soon as the fire starts burning. Those thin strips of kindling will often spark out small embers. Be particularly careful if you have children or pets in the house or anything flammable in front of the fire, like a rug.
9. Once the fire is well established and you're burning larger logs, you can put the fireguard to one side if you're staying in the room and can keep an eye on it. Put the guard back in front of the fire if you're leaving the room, even for a few moments.
10. Stop putting logs on the fire in the hour before heading to bed, and make sure the fire guard is in place before you leave the room for the night.

There are probably better techniques out there, but this is how I was taught when I was a teenager for our living room fire at home, and it works for me.

122

Safety lights at night

Having small, light-sensitive night lights in the kitchen, hallway and landing reduces the risk of people falling or tripping over things in the dark. Whether they're getting up to go to the kitchen, the bathroom or leaving very early for work.

They look like a plug with a small light fitting on top and they're cheap to run, coming on automatically at night when it's dark and turning off automatically at dawn when it's light again.

123

Preparing for potential power cuts

It's useful to have a small battery-powered storm lamp and a power bank that you can charge your phone from, to use during power cuts. Climate change is making our weather more unpredictable and we have more frequent storms.

If you get a storm warning on your local news or radio, you can make sure the lamp and power bank are charged up and ready, just in case. If you have one or more flasks that keep water hot, boil your kettle and fill them up so you can make a hot drink during a power cut, or fill a hot water bottle.

These are useful for people of any age, but particularly older relatives or friends living on their own. At least they know they'll be able to see to get around their home at night, get up and down the stairs, and to charge their phone and call someone if they need to.

124

Reducing electricity bills

If you want to take some of the sting out of your electricity bills, consider some or all of the following:

1. Make sure you're using LED bulbs in your ceiling lights and lamps. They're energy-efficient and long-lasting.
2. Use smart plugs to automatically turn your hallway, landing and living room lights on (at sunset) and off at the time you normally go to bed. They'll turn things off even if you forget.
3. Put a reminder on your phone to switch electricity supplier the day after your 12-month contract is up (or whenever your contract ends). There are websites that help you to switch that will do a lot of the legwork for you. It'll give you access to the best new customer discounts.
4. Choose an electricity plan that matches your electricity usage and lifestyle, e.g. cheap night rate, cheap EV rate or free electricity during part of the weekend.
5. If your electricity plan includes cheaper rates for certain hours, e.g. at night, you can charge things then and use the delay timer (and eco settings) on your dishwasher, washing machine and dryer (if they have that function) to set them to come on when your cheaper rate kicks in. Just make sure

your smoke and carbon monoxide alarms are working well. It will take you longer to respond to an appliance fire when you're asleep. It is generally safer to use these appliances while you're at home and awake.

6. Deal with energy vampires. Even if an appliance isn't in use right now, if it's plugged in, it's still using a small amount of electricity, e.g. to run the digital clock on the front of your cooker or microwave. The same applies to your toaster, kettle, coffee maker, hob, air fryer, lamps and phone or laptop chargers (even when unconnected to your phone or laptop). Things left on standby mode, like your TV, speaker or gaming console, use more electricity than you'd think. Over the course of a year, it adds up.
   - Turn them off at the plug or unplug them when not in use.
   - Or use a smart strip, which is a smart version of an extension lead with multiple power sockets and USB slots. Through its app, you can schedule things to automatically turn off at night.
7. Put a few tumble dryer balls in the drum when you're drying clothes, to reduce the drying time, if you can't dry outside. There are plastic versions and also wool versions if you'd like a more sustainable and slightly quieter option.
8. Only boil the amount of water you need in the kettle.
9. An air fryer uses a lot less electricity than running a larger, traditional oven.
10. Consider investing in photovoltaic (PV) panels and/or a battery, if that's an option. See the following chapter for more details.

125

If you're considering photovoltaic (PV) solar panels

They can reduce your electricity bills significantly, depending on the size of system you put in, plus it's an investment in renewable energy. If it's something you're considering, this may help you get started:

1. Check if there's a government grant for PV, whether you're eligible and what's required to get it. In Ireland there's a grant available from the SEAI. You'll need to apply for it before the PV system is installed and you'll need to get a new BER (Building Energy Rating) before the grant is paid. Getting a PV system generally improves your BER.
2. To work out what size of system you want, get an idea of your current annual kilowatt-hours (kWh) used, through your electricity supplier's online portal or bills. It'll be useful to be able to tell the PV suppliers that, when you start getting quotes. Depending on the number of panels you

get, a PV supplier can tell you roughly how many kWh that system will produce per year and what percentage of your current annual usage your PV system will cover.

3. Panels on south-facing roofs have the highest output. East- and west-facing panels also work well, even if they have slightly lower production than a south-facing system. Panels on north-facing roofs produce less than the other orientations but can still be useful if you're limited on where panels can go. The general consensus is to add as many panels as will fit on your roof, within your budget, to meet as much of your annual usage as possible.

4. An inverter is also needed, to convert the electricity generated from your panels (which is DC) to something your home can use (which is AC). There are two types of inverters, String and Hybrid. If you want a battery, either when you get the panels installed, or in the future, you'll need a hybrid inverter.

5. FIT = Feed In Tariff, the amount your electricity supplier will pay you for any unused electricity you send to the grid. Different countries will use different terms. In Ireland it's the CEG (Clean Export Guarantee). It will show as credits on your electricity bills. Credit built up over the summer can help offset the higher electricity bills incurred over winter. Note there may be tax to pay over a certain threshold, as it's classed as income.

6. Solar batteries are useful for storing unused solar electricity to use at another time. Plus, if you have access to cheaper night-rate electricity, you can charge your battery at night and use it to power your home for part of the following day. Batteries can undoubtably save you money, particularly in winter when PV panels are at their least productive, however they're quite expensive. You may decide that the savings from solar-powered electricity usage during the day, combined with the credits for what you sell back to your

supplier are enough for you. It's a matter of personal preference and budget.
7. You need a smart meter to get paid (accurately) for what you export to the grid. You don't have to change to a smart plan when you get a smart meter.
8. PV panels require daylight to work; it doesn't have to be sunny. As you'd expect, they don't produce as much during the winter. Depending on system size, they'll generally produce less than you need in winter, and more than you need in summer.
9. Panels tend to have a long lifespan of between 20-30 years, with a slight decline in efficiency over that time. An inverter lasts around 10-12 years so will need to be replaced at some stage.
10. Let your house insurer know if you've had PV panels installed. It won't necessarily affect your premium.

The above is what I wish I'd known at the start, when initially looking into this topic. I did invest in a PV system in the end and I'm really glad I did. Take the time to get a few quotes and check out the reviews of each supplier. Quotes for the same size of system can differ significantly. A reputable company won't put you under any pressure or demand full payment up front, and they'll be patient with your questions.

# 126

How much sun will your garden, terrace or balcony get?

If buying or renting a house or apartment and a sunny outside space is important to you, use a compass app on your phone when doing a property viewing to check which direction your outside space faces.

As long as you're not shaded by other buildings, walls, fences or mature trees, south-facing generally gets the most sun (morning and afternoon), east-facing will give you sun in the morning, west-facing will give you sun in the afternoon, while north-facing gets the least sun, but usually still some.

You can make a garden work in any of these orientations, if that's important to you, as there are plants that like a sunny spot and some that prefer shade.

127

A crash course in gardening

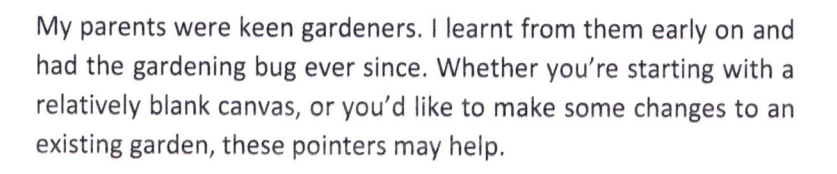

My parents were keen gardeners. I learnt from them early on and had the gardening bug ever since. Whether you're starting with a relatively blank canvas, or you'd like to make some changes to an existing garden, these pointers may help.

Types of plants and some lower-maintenance options

1. Evergreens keep their leaves all year long. Particularly useful in winter when the rest of the garden looks bare. Perennials come up in spring, stick around until winter, die right back, then come back in spring, for a few years. Annuals give you a burst of colour during the warmer months. They die back in winter and won't reappear the following spring. Deciduous refers to trees and shrubs that lose their leaves over winter and grow them back in spring.
2. Some plants need annual pruning (roses, lavender, etc.) but you can opt for low-maintenance plants if you don't fancy pruning. They'll just need monitoring, watering and the occasional feed.

3. Evergreens that don't need pruning (unless you want to reduce their size) include: Skimmia; Choisya; Phormium; Picea; Fatsia Japonica; Heather; Viburnum Davidii; Ceanothus; Nandina; Azalea; Mahonia; Bergenia; Ilex; Taxus Baccata and Aucuba.
4. Low-maintenance perennials include: Astrantia; Geranium Rozanne (or Renardii or Orion); Echinacea; Rudbeckia; Anemone (likely to spread); Hemerocallis; Salvia; Astilbe and Verbena Lollipop.
5. Good trees for small gardens include: Olea (Olive tree, plus it's evergreen); Prunus Amanogowa (tall, very narrow cherry); Prunus Pink Perfection; Amelanchier Alnifolia Obelisk; Magnolia Jane; Magnolia Stellata; Cotoneaster Hybridus Pendulus (evergreen); Malus Royal Beauty; Salix Caprea Kilmarnock; Sorbus Cashmiriana; Robinia Pseudoacacia Twisty Baby; Larix Kaempferi Stiff Weeper.

Garden planning and preparation

1. Have a think about how you'd like to use your garden, e.g. an area for BBQ and eating; somewhere for your children to play; a shady or sunny spot to read; space for a shed or garden room; and how much time you have to spend on maintenance. Consider the proportion of grass/artificial grass, patio and planted areas that you want.
2. If you're confident tackling the design yourself, then sketch it out on graph paper, or you can rope in a green-fingered friend or ask a professional garden designer.
3. Note where the sun is in the morning, mid-day and in the afternoon, to work out where you want to have your seating, in either sun or shade.
4. Flower beds look better when they're at least a metre wide, if you have the space. You can put them in along the outside edge of the garden, or include some larger square,

rectangular, round, L-shaped or kidney-shaped beds in the lawn or close to seating areas.

5. If you're creating a flower bed, use a garden hose to mark out the shape you want. Hose is flexible and easy to move around until you're happy with the shape, size and location. Use line-marking spray just inside the hose to mark the outline. Or use a spade to turn over the sods of earth along the edge of the bed.

6. If you're turning an area that was grass into a shrub or flower bed, one of the easiest ways is to cover the new bed with tarpaulin or similar, to block out the light for a few weeks until the grass is dead.

7. Once the grass is completely dead, empty some bags of compost across the top of the bed (roughly one bag per square metre) and do the same with a smaller amount of perlite. The first adds organic matter to the soil, the second improves drainage, particularly in clay.

8. Then dig up the bed to spade depth or a little deeper if you can, to mix the compost and perlite in really well. You can do this by hand or hire a rotovator if it's a larger area. When you can easily get your hand (up to the wrist) into the soil and wiggle your fingers, you're good to go. Prepping the bed properly gives your plants the best chance to thrive long-term.

9. For planting in pots, the smaller the pot, the more often it needs to be watered, so go big. Bigger pots are lower maintenance. And mix some Water Retention Gel into the compost to help it retain moisture.

10. If you're planning a big patio, leave a square or rectangular cut-out within it, so you can plant directly into that. It helps to break up a large block of hard landscaping. And put a raised edge around the patio, using kerbs, sleepers or similar, about 10cm higher than the patio, to help keep bark mulch in the flower beds, if they border the patio.

11. Some carefully placed solar lights as a finishing touch brings a garden to life at night.

Planting

1. The best time to plant a bed is autumn or spring, because plants won't need as much watering (than in the drier summer season) while getting established. But you can plant at any time as long as you're prepared to water when needed.
2. Choose sun- or shade-loving plants based on how much sun your planting areas get. Plant preferences for sun or shade are marked on the plant's label or pot. Same goes for hardiness. Buy things that can survive your worst-case winter temperatures.
3. Include a mix of evergreens, perennials (and annuals if you like them), and incorporate all heights – low, medium and tall. Having something tall (two to three metres or more) like a tree, will make a small space seem bigger. Try to choose things that flower at different times of the year (for you and the bees), including some spring-flowering bulbs like snowdrop, daffodil and tulip, which will come up year after year.
4. Choose your plants with the aim of planting in groups, using odd numbers, e.g. three of the same evergreen next to five of same perennial, next to three of a different evergreen, and one tree. Use complementary colours and shapes, e.g. three upright lance-shaped yellow plants look good behind five shorter, dome-shaped blue plants.
5. Put your plants (still in their pots until you're ready to plant) on top of the bed and move them around until you're happy with how it all looks. Put the tallest plants at the back or in the middle of the bed and the shortest things at the front.

6. Allow each plant enough space to grow to its mature size. Don't space them out based on their current size (unless you're doing a TV garden makeover and money is no object). They're only babies. If a plant's mature size (it should be on the label/pot) is one metre wide, give it one metre of space all to itself.
7. Once you like how it all looks (pre-planting), you can take things out of their pots and plant them. This will be quick and easy if you prepped the bed well. Scoop out a hole and pop them in (the top of the root ball should be the same height as the surrounding soil) and firm gently around them. If your planted bed looks extremely sparse to start with, that's how it should look. They'll fill the space much faster than you think.
8. When you're planting a tree, the thickest part of the trunk, just above the root system, needs to be above the ground. Put a stake in to support any trees for the first year or two. Hammer the stake into the soil at an angle, so it crosses the tree about a third of the way up the trunk, with the top of the stake pointing into the prevailing wind. Tie a rubber tree tie to the stake first, then to the tree.
9. Give everything a good watering after planting.

Aftercare

1. If you want to ditch most of the weeding for a year or two, put a four- to five-centimetre layer of bark mulch on the bed and top it up every couple of years. It keeps weeds down and moisture in.
2. If you find U-shaped notches on the edges of plant leaves, you have vine weevil. The adult beetles eat the leaves, but it's the grubs they lay in the soil that munch their way through plant roots from September to March, which can potentially kill plants. From early to late summer, if you go

outside occasionally when it's full dark, you can use a torch to find and get rid of the beetles. You'll find them on plants where you found those notches, and sometimes on nearby walls. They're particularly partial to potted plants. To deal with the grubs, there are specific products you can buy to pour on the soil but use with care to avoid adverse effects on other wildlife.
3. Give plants a feed at least once a year, at the start of the growing season. You can buy slow-release capsules to scatter on the soil, which last for a few weeks.
4. During any very sunny, warm weeks with no rain, you'll need to water your plants. And for trees, leave the hose near the base of the tree, on a low to medium flow rate, for 15-20 minutes (set a timer). Once per week should be fine in very dry weather.

The most important thing is, it's your garden, so put your stamp on the design – water features, gnomes, buddhas, tropical jungle or urban prairie, whatever makes you smile. Gardening is like painting in 3D.

128

Garden care over winter

When it comes to getting your garden ready for winter, and the associated wind, rain and frost (depending on where you live):

1. Bring anything that can get mouldy, like cushions or padded seats, inside, somewhere warm and dry.
2. Put small, fragile things like glass solar lights into the shed.
3. Recycled plastic furniture is one of the few types of furniture that can be left out all year, every year. You'll know you have this if it's chunky and very heavy compared to wooden or even metal furniture.
4. Otherwise, if you can't put garden furniture into a shed or garage, cover it with a waterproof furniture cover. Use bungee cords to secure the cover and stop strong winds blowing it off. Protecting your furniture over winter will prolong its life.
5. If you have large pots with tall plants that are likely to catch the wind and potentially topple over, you can use bungees to tie two or more pots together. The combined weight will make them much more stable. Just be careful with bungees (particularly if you have children or pets around). You don't want one snapping loose at high tension when you're attaching it.

6. Bring potted plants inside to a cool frost-free area if the plants are frost tender. If you have tender plants outside, you can also cover them with garden fleece during very cold snaps.
7. If your patio or decking tends to go green over winter, give it a good brush and then spray it in November with an anti-mould, moss and algae product. I use Wet & Forget.
8. Make sure you've fully emptied your power washer of any residual water in the system and then store it in a frost-free place.
9. Disconnect the spray gun at the end of your garden hose and bring it inside.
10. Spray a little WD-40 on the metal parts of garden tools, wipe off the excess and put them away.

129

Right for tight, left for loose

For opening and closing the lids on jars or putting the lid back on a bottle of water, my muscle memory kicks in and I don't have to think about it. But for things that I don't do every day, like turning on the tap outside to use the garden hose, or using an allen/hex key, this rhyme always helps.

130

Keep your bins inside your garden gate

Don't leave your waste, recycling or compost bins outside your garden gate unless it's bin-collection day. If it's an option, always store them inside your garden. Otherwise, you're just giving potential burglars something they can climb up on, to help them get over your garden gate or wall.

131

Selling your home

To increase the chance of selling your home and get the best price for it, you need to stage it, the same way interior designers do when they're setting up a show home in a new housing estate. You're aiming for as close to that look as you can get, using things you already have. You'll be making the most of things visually, and it doesn't generally require any big investment.

It's mostly a case of taking stuff away, choosing which things remain and making it look as attractive, large and neutral as possible.

In preparation for selling your home:

1. Ask friends, family or colleagues for recommendations on a solicitor (or attorney, depending on which country you live in) if you don't already have one. Let your solicitor know when you're planning to sell.
2. The best times to sell are spring and summer when days are brighter and people are out and about more.
3. Check your home's kerb appeal with fresh eyes. You don't need to repaint it (unless it really needs it), but you can pull weeds, clean the driveway, paint the front door if it's

looking tired, plant some flowers, add a window box or put a large container with shrubs and flowers out front. You can always take the window box and container with you when you move.
4. If there's a hedge or tree that is making some of your rooms very dark, consider getting that trimmed or cut back to let more light in (with your neighbour's consent if it's a shared boundary or their tree).
5. Inside, you need to de-personalise the house. Take down family photos, etc., and make it neutral, like a blank canvas, so that it looks inviting, but not like someone's already living there (like a show home). You want potential buyers to be able to imagine their things in your home, in their style.
6. Clean the inside and get rid of all clutter. Clear things off sideboards, mantles, coffee tables, windowsills, etc. Just have the odd ornament, plant and splash of colour. It'll also make each room seem bigger.
7. If you have any very dark colours on internal walls, ceilings or wood (panelling, skirting board or architrave), unless it was chosen by an interior decorator, paint it a light neutral colour – e.g. white, cream or pale grey. Lighter colours will give a sense of space. Same goes for wallpaper. Lightening the colours is one of the most effective things you can do to make each room look bigger.
8. Have a vase of fresh flowers on the dining table and set it fully with your nicest crockery, cutlery and wine glasses ready for viewing hours. You want buyers imagining having their friends over for dinner.
9. Colour is good but don't overdo it. If a bedroom has colourful curtains or headboard then complement that with a new plain white duvet cover and pillowcases. It'll also make the room feel bigger and calmer.

10. Make scent work for you. Bake cookies or bread on the morning before viewings. Or have a diffuser misting out some lemongrass oil in the hallway for an hour beforehand.
11. Take the advice of your estate agent or realtor when it comes to selling price. They'll know what similar properties in the area are selling for. Far better to price it competitively from the start and get people through the door and bidding, than to price it too high at the start and reduce the initial footfall. The longer your property is up for sale, the weaker your negotiating position. People start wondering why it hasn't sold and its perceived value drops. You want things moving along at a good pace, from initial marketing to completion.

Travel

132

An unapologetically nerdy packing list

Hopefully you've sorted your VISAs and vaccinations (if needed) a few weeks before your trip, checked in for any flights or other travel bookings and arranged parking.

Make sure to put your travel insurance emergency telephone number into your phone, along with your policy number. And send a screenshot of your digital boarding pass to someone else travelling with you (if you're not travelling solo), in case anything happens to your phone.

If, like me, you love a checklist, feel free to adopt and adapt this one for your typical packing and kind of holiday

1. Passport, flight boarding pass and any other travel tickets
2. Swimwear
3. Underwear
4. Clothing that you can mix and match including belts
5. Some mid-layers and something warmer for eating out at night or for early starts
6. Raincoat (can be one that packs up really small)

7. Cap or sunhat
8. Sunglasses and other glasses if you use them
9. Shoes and sandals
10. Suncream, deodorant, shampoo, other toiletries and cosmetics. Double-bag any liquids that are going in a check-in bag, in case they expand and leak in your case
11. Toothbrush, toothpaste and dental tape or floss
12. Shaver
13. Any medications you take
14. Insect repellent and Imodium, depending on where you're going
15. Ear plugs if noise in an unfamiliar place keeps you awake
16. Plug adaptors (if needed)
17. Charging cables for phones and other devices
18. Hair dryer (if the place you're staying doesn't have one), styling tools and brush
19. Headphones or earbuds
20. Small fold-up food shopping bag(s) if self-catering
21. Mini torch (depending on where you're going and the type of holiday)
22. Tea bags (if you're Irish, English or otherwise addicted to your favourite brew)
23. Address of the place you'll be staying
24. Home and car keys for your return trip
25. Check you don't have nail scissors or long metal nail files in your hand luggage or they'll most likely be confiscated

133

Making the most of the space in your liquids bag

If you're not bringing a check-in bag where you can pack your liquids, you'll want to make the most of the space in your one-litre liquids bag for carry-on luggage:

1. Bring a solid stick deodorant that you can put in your carry-on case, instead of a liquid one, freeing up space in your liquids bag.
2. Get a few of those small, circular, clear plastic containers with screw-on lids. They're about 2-3cm wide and less than 2cm high. You can get them on Amazon. You can fit enough facial moisturiser, serum or foundation in one of them to last a week. Don't overfill them or they may leak during the flight.
3. You can also buy small plastic bottles online (about 10cm tall and 2cm wide) to put your shampoo or conditioner in, which are much smaller than a shampoo bottle. Use a permanent marker to label what's in them.

4. There are travel-sized perfume or aftershave atomisers, which you can fill with your favourite scent.
5. You can always buy a couple of travel-sized toiletries at the chemist or drugstore in the airport after you've gone through security. They're small enough that you'll probably use most of them up during the holiday.

134

You can use a second liquids bag for prescription medicine

If you're only travelling with carry-on luggage and you're tight for space in your one-litre liquids bag, remember that if you have prescription medicine in liquid, gel or paste form, you're allowed to use a second one-litre liquids bag for that. I've never been asked to show my prescription, but it's a good idea to have it (or a copy or photo of it) somewhere easy to access, just in case.

135

Pack a Multi Charger Cable

Rather than bringing a few charging cables to cater for your different devices and ending up with a snake's nest of cables, just bring one Multi Charger Cable. A 'Four in One' or 'Three in One'. These have one USB-A charging cable, which plugs into a power socket or laptop, and attached to that are three or four different cable types, typically USB-C, Micro-USB and Lightning among others.

Because these are generally joined into one unit with many 'tails', they save you having to hunt under clothes for the one specific cable you're looking for.

Get one with a reasonably long cable as the place you're staying may not have plugs located close to where you'd like them.

136

Empty the bins

Before you go on holiday, make sure you've emptied any kitchen bins and compost caddies, to avoid coming home to stinky, mouldy bins. Particularly if you're going away for two weeks or more, and the weather is warm at home. I forgot once. It wasn't pretty. 'Nuff said.

137

Pre-holiday home security

Before you go on holiday, if you don't already have some, get a few smart plugs. You can set some lamps or the radio to turn on and off on a timed schedule (or more randomly), so it looks like someone's home.

Unplug your main appliances or turn them off at the socket. Your cooker, air fryer, microwave, dishwasher, washing machine, kettle, toaster, coffee maker, TV, game console, speakers, charger cables, etc. Anything that doesn't need to remain switched on. It will reduce the risk of fires, as well as reduce your electricity usage while you're away (things on standby still use power).

Don't leave waste or recycling bins outside the wall or gate into your garden if you have one, as it makes it easier for someone to access your garden and the back of your house.

If you have a trusted next-door neighbour, let them know you'll be away and ask them if they'll keep an eye on the place.

138

Final checklist before leaving home

1. Passport and tickets or boarding passes
2. Suitcases
3. Glasses and sunglasses
4. Phone
5. Bank cards
6. Car keys
7. Plants watered
8. No wet clothes in the washing machine
9. Kitchen bins and compost caddies emptied
10. Appliances that don't need to be left on are switched off at the socket or unplugged
11. Outside bins are inside the garden gate
12. Smart plugs are set up to turn things on and off
13. Windows closed and external doors locked
14. Home alarm on (if you have one)

139

Photograph your parking zone

If you're parking your car at the airport or a Park and Ride car park, before you walk away from it, take a photo of the zone or floor and row, or make a note of it on your phone. At least you'll know exactly where to find your car when you get back. This is for any of you who ever spent an hour looking for your car in a sea of cars when you got back from holiday. Once was enough for me.

140

Getting through airport security

Technology is improving all the time and different airports have slightly different systems or processes. But in general, to get through security as quickly and easily as possible, before you get to the conveyor belt, take your coat off, any loose-fitting hoodies or sweatshirts, chunky metal belts and footwear which is ankle-height (or higher) or has thick soles. Travelling in low-profile trainers, slip-ons or flip-flops is easier as you won't usually need to remove them.

Take keys or coins out of your pockets.

Have your liquids, pastes and gels to hand, in the airport's one-litre clear plastic bags, sealed, with no single item in it more than 100ml. You can use a second bag for prescription medicine if needed.

Put your laptop, tablet, eReader and any other electrical appliances in an outside pocket of your hand luggage so they're easy to access and place separately in a tray.

About the Author

Estelle Taylor is originally from Co. Donegal, Ireland, and is currently living in Co. Kildare, after one year in France, twelve years in the UK and fourteen years in Dublin.

She is Head of Communications for a large, multinational health business, which she describes as being her work family for the last seventeen years. Before that, she worked in a number of industries, including a few years in telecoms software, always in marketing and communications. She's been a people manager for twenty eight years.

Estelle is a keen gardener and reader, with a strong interest in health and holistic wellness.

Take back your strength and power,
with kindness,
and don't let anyone hold you back.
Don't just Be in the world.
Hold your head up and Shine.

Printed in Great Britain
by Amazon